FAKING THE NEWS

WHAT RHETORIC CAN TEACH US ABOUT DONALD J. TRUMP

Edited by
Ryan Skinnell, PhD

SOCIETAS
essays in political
& cultural criticism

imprint-academic.com

Published in the UK by
Imprint Academic Ltd., PO Box 200, Exeter EX5 5YX, UK

Distributed in the USA by
Ingram Book Company,
One Ingram Blvd., La Vergne, TN 37086, USA

ISBN 9781845409692 paperback

A CIP catalogue record for this book is available from the
British Library and US Library of Congress

Contents

Ryan Skinnell

Introduction to Faking the News

For anyone reading this book, Donald J. Trump is undoubtedly a familiar character. Whether you think his election to the US presidency in 2016 was a triumph or a tragedy, the man has been drawing crowds for decades.

Rhetoric, at least as we're using it in this book, is probably less familiar. For most people, rhetoric is the opposite of reality, summed up nicely by Teddy Roosevelt in 1917 when he wrote, "Rhetoric is a poor substitute for action, and we have trusted only to rhetoric. If we are really to be a great nation, we must not merely talk; we must act big."[1] As Roosevelt helpfully illustrates, rhetoric is often viewed as a form of linguistic deception—pretty or flattering language that disguises people's real intentions and misleads, or even tricks, audiences.

The definition of rhetoric as deception is useful, especially for understanding politicians. But it's also limited. Rhetoric specialists, more commonly called rhetoricians, study rhetoric in broader terms as "the art of persuasion in its various forms." As an area of study, rhetoric gives us a set of conceptual tools for studying persuasion. Rhetoric helps to make sense of the world by explaining how people use language (and other persuasive means) to get things done. Rhetoricians study deception, of course, but we also study how speakers and writers increase their authority, how they sway an audience, and how they convince people what to believe and/or how to act.

Rhetoric is not necessarily evil and deceptive, but it is *always* about how people use language, symbols, and gestures to accomplish (or to try to accomplish) their goals. Saying to your spouse "I need you to get milk at the store" is rhetorical because you are trying to get someone to do something. It may seem like a silly example, but actually convincing another person to buy you milk at the store is actually a pretty complex set of circumstances. It requires the presence of a relationship and of trust (you don't generally ask a stranger to buy you milk and bring it to your home). It requires shared knowledge (do you usually get whole milk or skim? Gallon or half gallon?). And it requires careful communication ("I need it for dinner, so please get it on your way home from work"). We take these complicated circumstances for granted, but the more you notice them, the more obvious it is that all human affairs really rely heavily on the effectiveness or not of these sorts of mundane interactions.

When people use language, the purpose is to achieve a particular outcome — whether it's getting milk, selling a product, appealing to voters, or taking a country to war. After all, achieving a goal is the whole point of persuasion, whether it's persuasion we think is good or persuasion we think is bad. People are constantly using language, symbols, and gestures to get other people to believe or act in certain ways. This is what rhetoric attempts to describe. As a result, studying rhetoric helps us understand a used car dealer's shady sales pitch as well as Nazi propaganda, but also the *Gettysburg Address* and the strategies scientists use to inform the public about new discoveries.

Rhetoric is actually one of Western Civilization's oldest arts. Aristotle wrote a textbook about it almost 2500 years ago. Chaucer, Shakespeare, and Milton all studied it in school. And John Quincy Adams taught it at Harvard in the early 1800s. For as long as formal schooling has existed in Europe and the United States, rhetoric has been a part of the curriculum in some form or fashion, and it still is.

After an extended period of being trapped in the odd college English or Speech-Communications class, the study of rhetoric is making a resounding comeback in the United States.

There are more than 70 PhD programs in rhetoric and an ever-growing number of undergraduate and Masters-level degree programs. Most people studying rhetoric in those programs are not (exclusively) studying deception, and the people teaching in rhetoric programs are certainly not teaching students how to be deceptive. Rather, the study of rhetoric is thriving in American colleges and universities because rhetoricians are helping students make sense of important persuasive phenomena in the world. The possibilities for studying persuasion are endless. They include social media and virality, globalization, marketing, technology, celebrity and pop culture, and, of course, national and international politics. Students encounter and practice thousands of different kinds of persuasion every day. Rhetoric gives them a particular set of skills for doing so thoughtfully.

Rhetoricians obviously think rhetoric's revival in higher education is important for helping students navigate an increasingly complex educational world. Students can access millions of conflicting sources on 20th-century Russian politics from their dorm rooms at 3:00am on any given day of the week. They can text or private message a struggling friend to set up a study date in the library. They can email a professor at a different university in another state with questions about a research project. And, they can teleconference with college students in Islamabad, Pakistan for a discussion on the benefits and drawbacks of cross-cultural art cooperatives. Understanding persuasion in each of these cases is really useful because it can help students make smart choices about how to accomplish their varying persuasive goals.

But, properly understood, rhetoric also has much to offer people who are not students or not just students. Rhetoric is closely linked to citizenship, democracy, and justice. That's why it has existed for thousands of years. Literally, the first rhetoric handbooks were written to help citizens in Ancient Greece participate in the first democracy.

Persuasion plays a particularly important role in democracies because of how central it is to making the government work. Politicians have to persuade voters, policymakers have to persuade members of other parties, lawyers have to persuade jurors, and citizens have to contribute to all of those processes in various ways. In dictatorships, decisions do not require any input beyond the dictator's. But in democracies, citizens have to participate knowledgeably in the government to make it work. Which means, they need to understand how persuasion works and how to be persuasive. Being an active member of a democracy requires citizens (as well as non-citizens, for that matter) to understand how other people are attempting to inform, motivate, and persuade them — for good or ill. How do you know which candidate to vote for? How should you evaluate evidence if you're on a jury? What are the possible effects of a ballot measure or a proposition? Knowing these things helps people make better choices.

It's obviously possible to learn about persuasion without learning about rhetoric, just as it's possible to learn how to make delicious, seven-course meals without taking a cooking class. But a cooking class can help you understand and develop useful techniques for throwing a dinner party. Likewise, rhetoric can help by giving names to common persuasive tactics, by developing practical systems for assessing arguments and evidence, and by teaching people to see how persuasion works in general, as well as in more specific cases.

The goal of *Faking the News: What Rhetoric Can Teach Us about Donald J. Trump*, then, is to try to make sense of how the world works in the wake of Donald J. Trump's election as the 45th President of the United States of America.

It will become pretty clear pretty quickly that the contributors to this book find President Trump's election troubling. There are many reasons why, but the ones we are qualified to make sense of are rhetorical: how did a man who routinely lied to reporters and to his supporters, who called his opponents names and insulted voters, who made crass comments about women and immigrants and many others, and who obviously and proudly had no grasp of US policy get himself elected? How did he establish authority? How did he sway audiences?

And how did he convince people that he was qualified, capable, and responsible enough to deserve their votes?

Obviously, people have asked these questions at least since his infamous ride down the elevators at Trump Towers in June 2015 to announce his candidacy. And we've read some really compelling answers in the years since—written by academics, journalists, and cultural commentators alike. But these are still open questions.

In the following pages, eleven well-respected rhetoricians from around the US address the question of what rhetoric can teach us about Donald J. Trump. Each chapter (there are ten plus an afterword) is written for readers who may or may not know anything about the study of rhetoric. The chapters are roughly organized to move from more politically oriented subject matter to more identifiably pop culture oriented subjects, but given the main focus of the book, those distinctions don't hold up very well. However, the chapters are also intended to stand alone. In other words, they do not need to be read in any particular order. Readers should feel free to dip in and out as they see fit.

Each chapter takes a unique angle on Trump—for example, analyzing his persuasive uses of antisemitism or his television habits. The authors' goal in each case is to explain a little bit about rhetoric and help readers understand what rhetoric teaches us about Trump. Specifically, about how he uses language, symbols, gestures, and even style to appeal to the people in his various audiences and/or how other people in the world use language, symbols, gestures, and even style to make claims about Trump.

After reading *Faking the News: What Rhetoric Can Teach Us about Donald J. Trump*, we think readers will be better able to understand how a person like Trump in general, and how Donald J. Trump in particular, has come to power. We think readers will develop new tools for understanding the news, the administration, and the world. And we also think—or at least we hope—readers will be better positioned to assess, and if necessary oppose, bad actors in the future. This means Trump, but it also means anyone who sets out to persuade us to believe or act against our best interests. Of course, this book won't teach readers everything there is to know about Trump, about rhetoric, or about persuasion. And even if it could, rhetoric isn't a silver bullet. But it is still a powerful tool, and one that has been put to good use in strengthening democracy for more than two millennia. We expect readers will put it to good use for years to come.

I will end here with a brief note about the contributors. They are all trained rhetoricians with PhDs from nationally recognized rhetoric programs. They are all professors of rhetoric. They have all produced substantial academic scholarship—between them, they've written or edited 30 books, won several major national grants, and published an untold number of articles, essays, and book chapters. Some have written about Trump for national media outlets, including *The Conversation*, *Huffington Post*, *Politico*, *ProPublica*, *USA Today*, *Washington Monthly*, and *The Washington Post*. Others have written extensively about presidential rhetoric, demagoguery, technology, and language and politics in academic venues.

Some of the contributors' many accomplishments are described at the end of the book, and I encourage readers to read what each has done. But in all cases, they are highly qualified public intellectuals, and, maybe more importantly, highly motivated to understand Trump as a rhetorical creature. And even more importantly, they are writing for readers who are motivated to do the same with the hope that we can (re)build America into a better democracy than it is today.

Notes

1　Theodore Roosevelt, *The Foes of Our Own Household* (New York: George H. Doran Company, 1917), 40.

Michael J. Steudeman

Demagoguery
and the Donald's
Duplicitous Victimhood

In July of 2015, Texas Governor Rick Perry — then one of sixteen contenders for the Republican presidential nomination — issued a condemnation of rival Donald J. Trump. He insisted that Trump's campaign, with its anti-immigrant rhetoric and attacks on fellow politicians, represented a "toxic mix of demagoguery, mean-spiritedness, and nonsense."[1] Trump's response, predictably, relied on all of the rhetorical strategies Perry condemned as "demagogic." He made fun of Perry's eye-glasses and chastised the Texan for failing to keep Mexican "criminals" from crossing the state border.[2] At the same time, Trump cast doubt on Perry's accusation by attacking its ambiguity. Perry, he said, "doesn't understand what the word demagoguery means."[3]

Though Americans have a long history of calling their political adversaries "demagogues," during the 2016 campaign the term was revitalized by people struggling to make sense of Trump's abrupt ascendancy.[4] Countless authors, pundits, politicians, and scholars have echoed Perry's charge.[5] For scholars of communication, this resurgence of the term "dema-gogue" demands a moment's critical reflection. The meaning of the word is notoriously murky. Often, people use "dema-gogue" to refer to a speaker they dislike who happens to use unethical arguments.[6] This usage weakens the value of the term, making it easy for a demagogic politician to deflect the accusation—for instance, by saying an opponent doesn't know what the word means.

Instead, rhetorical scholar Patricia Roberts-Miller argues, it is more productive to think of demagoguery as a form of argument that emphasizes in-group identity to avoid the complexities of policy and the challenges of democratic deliberation.[7] In demagogic argument, reasoning is all about who belongs in the tribe. Any effort to compromise, or acknowledge the shared humanity of the out-group, in turn seems unreasonable. The traditional demands of democracy—acknowledging nuance, making sacrifices, living with difference—become threatening. For Roberts-Miller, shifting focus from *demagogues* to *demagogic argument* has important advantages. Focusing on the *person* mistakes symptom for cause, pinpointing evildoers rather than addressing the problems of civic culture that made demagoguery compelling to audiences in the first place. More fundamentally, thinking about demagogues in terms of bad versus good people is, itself, a demagogic way of thinking. A focus on arguments helps us notice when *we* are the ones getting duped.

Under this argument-centric definition, what matters is not whether Trump is a demagogue, but rather how his rhetoric operates demagogically. Trump's rhetoric is centered on the preservation of a conception of American identity rooted in whiteness, masculinity, and heteronormativity. He makes sweeping condemnations of media, politicians, and public figures based on their perceived alignment with progressive, liberal, or Democratic causes. He practices what Roberts-Miller calls "naïve realism," offering up a worldview of simple truths and falsehoods.[8] He minimizes the complexity of public problems and exaggerates his capacity to solve them. Many authors in this book highlight these various facets of Trump's rhetoric. In this chapter, I argue that a duplicitous claim of victimhood lies at the heart of Trump's demagoguery. Exploring the allure and resilience of Trump's victimhood appeal, I discuss some strategies rhetorical scholars recommend for undermining such a deceptive posture of pain.

Demagoguery and Victimhood

Trump portrays himself as uniquely besieged by larger forces. Throughout the Republican primaries, he complained of unfair treatment by the Republican National Committee, by debate moderators, and by the media.[9] During the general election, he said that the IRS unfairly targeted him for audits and that the election itself was "rigged" for his opponent.[10] Once he arrived in the White House, he claimed his administration spokespeople and his family received "very unfair" coverage from the press.[11] In a May 2017 speech, he went so far as to proclaim that "No politician in history—and I say this with great surety—has been treated worse or more unfairly."[12] Trump's persona seems to rely on projections of strength, masculinity, and—as he put it—"stamina."[13] Yet he presents himself as thin-skinned, even *whiny*, in the face of common political and presidential challenges. How do these claims of victimhood fit into Trump's broader demagogic appeal?

In the most straightforward sense, the demagogue's victimhood and strength have a complementary relationship. After all, a person has to be "under siege" in order to plausibly fend off enemies on all sides. Take the example of Louisiana's notorious demagogue, Governor Huey Long. As rhetoric scholar Joshua Gunn writes, Long's rhetoric generated a relationship between a helpless audience and himself, "a superhuman impervious to attack."[14] To create this dynamic, Long emphasized the unique difficulties that he faced as a politician by, for instance, stressing his readiness to ward off would-be assassins with a pistol. The portrayal of superhuman strength, then, required the conjuring of uncommon obstacles. Similarly, Trump's talk of a "rigged" system and "unfair" media reinforced supporters' sense that he overcame challenges no other politician had to face. Encouraging his audience to join in his parade of grievances, he constructed himself as the only person equipped to fight back.

Trump's invitation to victimhood, in turn, became a way for his constituency to identify with him. Paul Elliott Johnson, among the first rhetorical scholars to publish an account of

Trump's demagoguery, situates victimhood at the heart of the Donald's appeal. "Demagogues encourage audiences to self-identify as victims on the basis of *felt* precarity," Johnson explains, "encouraging the well-off and privileged to adopt the mantle of victimhood at the expense of those who occupy more objectively fraught positions."[15] In other words, Trump asks his audience to share his feelings that the world is unfair and set up to harm them, even if those feelings have no basis in material reality. This, in turn, motivates them to put their faith in the speaker and withdraw from the risks of democratic pluralism.

In Trump's discourse, the victims are white men rooted in a set of normative values often associated with 1950s America. Their way of life is purportedly eroded by forces of cultural difference (feminism, religious pluralism, the academic left, LGBTQ movements, racial justice protests, immigrants, and so on), all of which are catered to by the establishment Trump frames as his enemy. Though often framed as the "economically anxious," the persistence of white male support for Trump across lines of class suggests that their grievances were mainly racial, gendered, and cultural—not economic.[16]

By appealing to victimhood, Trump intensified a longtime strand of right-wing politics. In his study of the "politics of resentment" in the United States, Jeremy Engels traces the particular brand of divisiveness back to the presidency of Richard Nixon.[17] Like Trump, Nixon regularly complained of mistreatment by the media and institutions.[18] Also like Trump, Nixon parlayed that sense of personal grievance into a wider appeal to a "silent majority" victimized by a "vocal minority" of disruptive protesters, civil rights advocates, and others threatening "law and order."

While both Nixon and Trump exhibited these demagogic tendencies, there is a crucial difference between them. As I have argued elsewhere, Nixon often went to great lengths to present himself as worldly, experienced, informed, and inclusive—at least on the surface. He appealed regularly to the rhetorical trope of irony, stepping away from the partisan rancor to position himself as a reasonable figure above the fray.[19] With Trump, the demagogic core of seething resentment is always front-and-center in his arguments.

It is through the rhetoric of victimhood that Trump converts issues of policy into questions of identity. Consider, for instance, the way he advocated for a Republican plan to repeal the Affordable Care Act. Even as members of Congress struggled to defend their plan to the public, Trump concentrated on the grievances of those who resented the legislation. Opening a speech on health care in Milwaukee, he gestured to two families who represented "millions of people who have been victimized by Obamacare, a terrible law." Offering no specifics on the Republican proposal to repeal and replace the bill, Trump framed any opposition in terms of party tribalism rather than policy differences. "If it's the greatest health care plan ever devised," he said, "we will get zero votes by the obstructionists, the Democrats."[20] In Trump's demagogic appeal, enacting a repeal of the ACA was more about getting revenge on an out-group, the Democrats, than constructing a viable policy to improve Americans' lives.

At its most extreme, Trump's appeals to victimhood turn to scapegoating. In this type of appeal, the many grievances afflicting the in-group are pinned on some enemy. The only solution is to expel that enemy from the body politic.[21] Particularly in his stances toward Mexican immigrants and Muslims, Trump expresses this logic of social purification. Take his June 2017 speech in Cedar Rapids, Iowa, in which he cherry-picked an example to make a (demonstrably false) argument that undocumented immigrants commit more crimes than anyone else in the United States.[22] Proclaiming a vast epidemic, he implored that immigrants' "victims have been ignored" by "the media," "the consultants," and "by Washington." Turning to a language of expulsion, he concluded with a promise to capture "these gang members, these drug dealers, thieves, robbers, predators, criminals, killers, horrible killers, and [throw] them the hell out of our country."[23] In the end, Trump's appeal to victimhood rationalizes virtually any act of violence against the out-group. After all, the demagogic logic goes, they would kill us if they had the chance.[24]

A Rhetoric of Reversal

Many have recognized the language of white male grievance in Trump's rhetoric and called it what it is: demagoguery. Yet Trump's claims of victimhood, especially on behalf of his supporters, have a slippery quality that makes them difficult to question, let alone dispel. Jennifer Mercieca, the author of a forthcoming book on Trump's demagoguery, explains that Trump uses a range of logical fallacies to sidestep allegations of unethical rhetoric. For instance, he appeals to *ad populum* (the wisdom of the crowd), *ad baculum* (threats), and *ad hominem* (personal attacks) to deflect critique.[25] Of all Trump's demagogic defense mechanisms, among the most illuminating is his rhetoric of reversal, an approach that appropriates and inverts others' claims of hardship. Through its reliance on false equivalency, Trump's reversals are calibrated to insulate his appeal to victimhood.

To appreciate the challenge posed by Trump's rhetoric of reversal, it is necessary to recognize that a claim of victimhood is a claim of pain. And a claim of pain is, in the liberal discourse of the United States, conceived as unassailable. As cultural theorist Lauren Berlant asserts, assertions of pain are treated as "universally *intelligible*, constituting objective evidence of trauma."[26] As a consequence, "feeling *bad* becomes evidence for a structural condition of injustice" while "feeling *good* becomes evidence of justice's triumph."[27] The problem is that how one *feels* is a closed-off mental state, yet treated as unquestionable proof of hardship. As a result, when two claims of pain are set side-by-side, it is possible to draw false equivalencies between them. As rhetorical scholar Patricia G. Davis says, it only takes a short leap from this equivocation to decide that "*claims* of racism, rather than racism itself... inflict injury upon those who are accused of racist behavior."[28]

Drawing from these unassailable claims, Trump's rhetoric of victimhood is upheld by such false equivocations. Consider, for instance, his early campaign attacks on Fox News anchor Megyn Kelly, particularly after the Republican candidate debate in August 2015. For a month afterward, controversy surrounded Trump's claim that Kelly's assertive debate questioning was due to the "blood coming out of her wherever."[29] Reacting to charges of sexism, Trump tweeted: "Do you ever notice that lightweight @megynkelly constantly goes after me but when I hit back it is totally sexist."[30] Implied in the claim is that Trump and Kelly were playing on an equal field, both "going after" each other, and that Kelly was given a privileged latitude to attack Trump because she was a woman. Trump, in turn, became the victim of unfair treatment.

Throughout his campaign and presidency, Trump has adopted a similar approach toward race and religion, positioning himself and his supporters as victims of "political correctness." The rhetoric of reversal plays a particularly potent role in Trump's appeals to "law and order." Part of Trump's appeal to his base was an objection to efforts by groups like Black Lives Matter to challenge police brutality and mass incarceration. (In one address he outright encouraged police to be needlessly rough to untried suspects.[31]) Turning those groups' legitimate grievances against them, he instead defined the *allegation* of racist policing as itself a form of "unfair defamation and vilification" responsible for "hostility and violence" toward police.[32] If you discuss crime in America's cities, he remarked at an October 2016 campaign event, "they say bad things about you. They call you a racist."[33] Being accused of racism is, Trump suggests, worse than being subjected to it.

For those hoping to contest Trump's demagoguery, his reversible arguments prove frustrating to address. The impulse is to charge him with hypocrisy: to point out that he is guilty of precisely the behaviors he condemns, or that he encourages his in-group to enact the same behaviors as the hated out-group. The downside to charging hypocrisy is that, by itself, it only reifies the tit-for-tat logic of demagogic argument. Calling Trump a hypocrite means charging him with doing exactly what his adversaries do. But the fact that his adversaries do it

gives him a pass to do it, too. This is why Trump so unapolo-
getically uses the *tu quoque* fallacy—Latin for "and you, too"—
that deflects allegations back upon the accuser. Caught on tape
discussing acts of sexual assault, Trump doubled down on the
infidelities of President Bill Clinton.[34] Lambasted for pardoning
Sheriff Joe Arpaio, Trump countered that Clinton issued a
controversial pardon of Marc Rich.[35] In a demagogic logic
predicated on victimhood, there is no need to defend a controversial action. All is fair so long as the ledger is balanced.

When a Witch Hunt Isn't a Witch Hunt: Debunking Duplicity

By any measure, Trump's claims of victimhood are duplicitous.
He was born into substantial wealth.[36] He received billions of
dollars in free campaign coverage from the major news outlets
he so often maligns.[37] He never substantiated his claims of
election rigging or IRS targeting. He holds the most vaunted
office in the nation, despite absolutely no background in
government or public service. Yet through his demagogic
rhetoric, he has constructed a victimized persona that resonates
with a resentful constituency. The slippery, reversible nature of
Trump's appeals to victimhood makes them incredibly difficult
to refute. Despite that, rhetorical scholars have developed
certain critical tools to help reveal these duplicitous elements of
Trump's demagoguery.

First, a demagogue's assertion of victimhood can often be
illustrated by attending closely to the discourse itself for
evidence of duplicity. As rhetorical scholar Robert Asen argues,
texts can contain markers of access, wealth, and privilege that
belie their speakers' claims of "outsider" status and
oppression.[38] For example, in a controversial speech at the Boy
Scouts of America's annual Jamboree, Trump went on a
lengthy tangent about his repeated interactions with famed real
estate mogul William Levitt at wealthy New York parties
attended by "a lot of successful people." Trump's goal was to
frame Levitt as an example of the "forgotten man" in American
life. That goal was undermined by his choice to tell an audience

of children about his experiences hanging out at millionaire galas.[39]

Secondly, duplicity can also be exposed by considering the way a demagogue appropriates a term to claim their victimhood. Take Trump's repeated claim that the investigation of his campaign's possible collusion with Russia is a "witch hunt."[40] As scholars Robert Ivie and Oscar Giner explain, the term "witch hunt" has long referred to instances in which "others" in a community have been scapegoated in response to visceral fears. Typically, the accused already suffered from diminished power. In Salem, women accused of witchcraft were poor, disowned, or enslaved, and thus unable to seek recourse against allegations. In the "Red Scare" of the 1950s, there was a disparity of power between accusers like Senator Joseph McCarthy and the artists, teachers, and actors they targeted. In the xenophobia that followed 9/11, the victims of "witch hunts" were religious and ethnic minorities.[41] Contrasting these past "witch hunts" with the billionaire president's claim helps to demonstrate the exaggerated nature of his victimhood claim.

Unfortunately, these two strategies reach a crucial limit. For supporters who identify with Trump's perspective, discounting of their feelings of victimhood—however unsubstantiated they may be—reinforces their attraction to the demagogue. To be sure, revealing Trump's personal duplicity can help undermine his appeal among those who view him as a spokesperson for working class interests. Alone, though, this approach threatens to reify resentments among those who already identify with Trump by implying that their own feelings are not genuine. That is why it is more essential to resist the demagogue's game altogether—to reframe the discourse in ways that emphasize policy.

Claims of victimhood can be contested by focusing on the *ends* of discourse. Demagogic argument tries to turn everything into a matter of identity. As Roberts-Miller argues, the challenge is to turn the discourse back to matters of policy and concrete outcomes.[42] In this argumentative pivot, the argument ceases to be about getting revenge on an out-group. Instead, the conversation becomes about how to alleviate people's material challenges. For instance, consider Trump's repeated appeals that Americans were "victims" of Obamacare. With the law framed as an attempt to deliberately harm his supporters, the only solution was to repeal the law and get revenge on those who passed it. In 2017, as Senate Republicans pushed to actually repeal components of Obamacare, public conversation emphasized the material consequences of Trump's touted policy. With a discourse predicated on improving lives rather than affirming victimhood, public opinion intensified in opposition to repeal.[43] As Wendy Brown would put it, the wounded "language of 'I am'" was momentarily supplanted by a more productive discourse of "I want this for us."[44]

Obviously, this technique is a small solace in the face of a demagogue in a position of considerable institutional power. Ultimately, truly contesting Trump's claims to victimhood will require that he lose the sanction of media and political institutions. As James Darsey contends, the demagogic force of Joseph McCarthy relied on his use of the institutional authority of the Senate. The chamber's decision to censure him in 1954 signaled to the public "that he no longer participated in the collective ethos of that body," thus undermining the credibility of his baseless accusations.[45] Trump's duplicity will be harder to contest, in part because the sources that sanction his appeals to victimhood are far more diffuse. He draws authority from Fox News, the ethos of the White House, the megaphone of social media, a Republican Party that rebukes him in word but not in deed, and a vast array of online media that reinforce the rhetoric of white male grievance. These sources, foundational to Trump's credibility, seem less likely to stand against him than those Senators who censured McCarthy sixty years ago.

Nonetheless, it is incumbent on all of those in positions of institutional authority to be wary of giving voice to Trump's discourse of victimhood. Not all claims of suffering are equal. Not all grievances deserve the same hearing. Not all pain can be traced back to concrete conditions of material hardship. To escape Trump's rhetoric of resentment, it is necessary to affirm these premises and declare that revenge is not a coherent political program.

Notes

1   Stephen Collinson, "Is Donald Trump a Demagogue?" *CNN.com*, July 23, 2015, http://www.cnn.com/2015/07/23/politics/donald-trump-rick-perry-demagogue/index.html.

2   Jeremy Diamond, "Donald Trump vs. Rick Perry: The Social Media Battlefront," *CNN.com*, July 22, 2015, http://www.cnn.com/2015/07/22/politics/donald-trump-rick-perry/index.html.

3   Donald J. Trump, Twitter post, July 16, 2015, https://twitter.com/realdonaldtrump/status/621783444083884037.

4   On the history of "demagoguery" as a concept in American public life, see Michael Signer, *Demagogue: The Fight to Save Democracy from Its Worst Enemies* (New York: St. Martin's Press, 2009).

5   Megan Garber, "What We Talk About When We Talk About Demagogues," *The Atlantic*, December 10, 2015, https://www.theatlantic.com/entertainment/archive/2015/12/what-we-talk-about-when-we-talk-about-demagogues/419514/; "Democratic Activist Says Donald Trump Fits Demagogue Mold," *NPR Morning Edition*, December 9, 2015, https://www.npr.org/2015/12/09/459026263/democratic-activist-says-donald-trump-fits-the-mold-of-a-demagogue; Jennifer Mercieca, "The Rhetorical Brilliance of Trump the Demagogue," *The Conversation*, December 11, 2015, http://theconversation.com/the-rhetorical-brilliance-of-trump-the-demagogue-51984.

6   Patricia Roberts-Miller, *Demagoguery and Democracy* (New York: The Experiment, 2017), 24; J. Michael Hogan and Dave Tell, "Demagoguery and Democratic Deliberation: The Search for Rules of Discursive Engagement," *Rhetoric & Public Affairs* 9.3 (2006): 479–487; James Darsey, "Patricia Roberts-Miller, Demagoguery, and the Troublesome Case of Eugene Debs," *Rhetoric & Public Affairs* 9.3 (2006): 463–470.

7   Roberts-Miller, *Demagoguery and Democracy*, 33.

8   Patricia Roberts-Miller, "Dissent as 'Aid and Comfort to the Enemy': The Rhetorical Power of Naïve Realism and Ingroup Identity," *Rhetoric Society Quarterly* 39.2 (2009): 170–188.

9   Peter W. Stevenson, "18 Times Donald Trump Complained about Being Treated Unfairly," *Washington Post*, April 19, 2016, https://www.washingtonpost.com/news/the-fix/wp/2016/04/19/18-times-donald-trump-complained-about-being-treated-unfairly/?utm_term=.c356e7b90983.

10   Eugene Scott, "Trump Says He Gets 'Unfairly' Audited by the IRS," *CNN.com*, February 27, 2016, http://www.cnn.com/2016/02/27/politics/donald-trump-irs-audit/index.html; Jonathan Martin and Alexander Burns, "Officials Fight Donald Trump's Claim of a Rigged Vote," *New York Times*, October 16, 2016, https://www.nytimes.com/

2016/10/17/us/politics/donald-trump-election-rigging.html.

[11] "Jeanine Pirro Interviews Donald Trump at the White House," *Fox News*, May 13, 2017, https://www.youtube.com/watch?v=jlWws-jd9qg&t=605.

[12] Donald Trump, "Remarks by President Trump at United States Coast Guard Academy Commencement Ceremony," *The White House: Office of the Press Secretary*, May 17, 2017, https://www.whitehouse.gov/the-press-office/2017/05/17/remarks-president-trump-united-states-coast-guard-academy-commencement.

[13] Amanda Hess, "What's Really Behind Trump's Obsession With Clinton's 'Stamina?'" *New York Times Magazine*, October 11, 2016, https://www.nytimes.com/2016/10/16/magazine/whats-really-behind-trumps-obsession-with-clintons-stamina.html.

[14] Joshua Gunn, "Hystericizing Huey: Emotional Appeals, Desire, and the Psychodynamics of Demagoguery," *Western Journal of Communication* 71 (2007): 17.

[15] Paul Elliott Johnson, "The Art of Masculine Victimhood: Donald Trump's Demagoguery," *Women's Studies in Communication* 40.3 (2017): 230.

[16] Eric Sasson, "Blame Trump's Victory on College-Educated Whites, Not the Working Class," *New Republic*, November 15, 2016, https://newrepublic.com/article/138754/blame-trumps-victory-college-educated-whites-not-working-class.

[17] Jeremy Engels, *The Politics of Resentment: A Genealogy* (University Park: Penn State University Press, 2015).

[18] This theme runs throughout Rick Perlstein, *Nixonland: The Rise of a President and the Fracturing of America* (New York: Scribner, 2000).

[19] Michael J. Steudeman, "Entelechy and Irony in Political Time: The Preemptive Rhetoric of Nixon and Obama," *Rhetoric & Public Affairs* 16.1 (2013): 59–96.

[20] Donald J. Trump, "President Trump Remarks on Health Care," *C-SPAN.org*, June 13, 2017, https://www.c-span.org/video/?429917-1/president-trump-delivers-remarks-health-care.

[21] Kenneth Burke, *The Philosophy of Literary Form: Studies in Symbolic Action*, 3rd Ed. (Berkeley: University of California Press, 1974), 202–205.

[22] Jane C. Timm, "Fact Check: No Evidence Undocumented Immigrants Commit More Crimes," *NBC News*, June 28, 2017, https://www.nbcnews.com/politics/white-house/fact-check-no-evidence-undocumented-immigrants-commit-more-crimes-n777856.

[23] Donald J. Trump, "President Trump Remarks in Iowa," *C-SPAN*, June 21, 2017, https://www.c-span.org/video/?430256-1/president-trump-urges-gop-add-money-health-care-bill.

[24] Roberts-Miller, *Demagoguery and Democracy*, 81–83.

[25] Mercieca, "The Rhetorical Brilliance of Trump the Demagogue."

[26] Lauren Berlant, "The Subject of True Feeling: Pain, Privacy, and

Politics," in *Cultural Pluralism, Identity Politics, and the Law*, edited by Austin Sarat (Ann Arbor: University of Michigan Press, 1999), 72; Wendy Brown, *States of Injury: Power and Freedom in Late Modernity* (Princeton, NJ: Princeton University Press, 1995), 52–76.

27 Berlant, "The Subject of True Feeling," 58.

28 Patricia G. Davis, "Reversal of Injury in the Obama Era: *Shelby County v. Holder*, Ressentiment, Moral Authority, and the Discursive Construction of White Victimhood," *Rhetoric Review* 36.4 (2017): 320–331.

29 Holly Yan, "Donald Trump's 'Blood' Comment about Megyn Kelly Draws Outrage," *CNN.com*, August 8, 2015, http://www.cnn.com/2015/08/08/politics/donald-trump-cnn-megyn-kelly-comment/index.html.

30 Donald J. Trump, Twitter post, September 22, 2015, https://twitter.com/realdonaldtrump/status/646504336940531712.

31 Philip Bump, "Trump's Speech Encouraging Police to be 'Rough,' Annotated," *Washington Post*, July 28, 2017, https://www.washingtonpost.com/news/politics/wp/2017/07/28/trumps-speech-encouraging-police-to-be-rough-annotated/?utm_term=.5307e5c960a6.

32 Donald J. Trump, "Remarks by President Trump at the 36th Annual Peace Officers' Memorial Service," *The White House: Office of the Press Secretary*, May 15, 2017, https://www.whitehouse.gov/the-press-office/2017/05/15/remarks-president-trump-36th-annual-national-peace-officers-memorial.

33 Donald J. Trump, "Donald Trump in Colorado Springs, CO," *Factbase*, October 18, 2016, https://factba.se/transcript/donald-trump-speech-colorado-springs-co-october-18-2016.

34 Eli Stokols and Madeline Conway, "Trump Hosts Surprise Panel with Bill Clinton's Accusers," *Politico*, October 9, 2016, https://www.politico.com/story/2016/10/donald-trump-bill-clinton-accusers-229441.

35 "Remarks by President Trump and President Niinistö of Finland in Joint Press Conference," *The White House: Office of the Press Secretary*, August 28, 2017, https://www.whitehouse.gov/the-press-office/2017/08/28/remarks-president-trump-and-president-niinist%C3%B6-finland-joint-press.

36 Zoe Thomas, "How Did Donald Trump Make His Fortune?" *BBC News*, April 13, 2016, http://www.bbc.com/news/business-35836623.

37 Nate Silver, "How Trump Hacked the Media," *FiveThirtyEight*, March 30, 2016, https://fivethirtyeight.com/features/how-donald-trump-hacked-the-media/.

38 Robert Asen, "Ideology, Materiality, and Counterpublicity: William E. Simon and the Rise of a Conservative Counterintelligentsia," *Quarterly Journal of Speech* 95.3 (2009): 263–288.

39 Donald J. Trump, "Remarks by President Trump at the 2017 National Scout Jamboree," *WhiteHouse.gov*, July 24, 2017, https://www.white

house.gov/the-press-office/2017/07/24/remarks-president-trump-2017-national-scout-jamboree.

40   "Excerpts from Trump's Conversation with Journalists on Air Force One," *New York Times*, July 13, 2017, https://www.nytimes.com/2017/07/13/us/politics/trump-air-force-one-excerpt-transcript.html.

41   Robert L. Ivie and Oscar Giner, "Hunting the Devil: Democracy's Rhetorical Impulse to War," *Presidential Studies Quarterly* 37.4 (2007): 580–598.

42   Roberts-Miller, *Demagoguery and Democracy*, 18–20.

43   Perry Bacon, Jr., "Why the Senate's Obamacare Repeal Failed," *FiveThirtyEight*, July 28, 2017, https://fivethirtyeight.com/features/why-obamacare-repeal-failed/.

44   Brown, *States of Injury*, 75.

45   James Darsey, "Joe McCarthy's Fantastic Moment," *Communication Monographs* 62 (1995): 79.

Anna M. Young

Rhetorics of Fear and Loathing: Donald Trump's Populist Style

When I agreed to be on the conference panel that led to this chapter and this book, I thought it would be an opportunity to reflect on what has to be the most turbulent and exhausting political experience of any presidential campaign in my lifetime, at least to date. I thought we would be looking back, in other words. Having to reckon with the subject of Donald Trump as president on a minute-by-minute basis across a spectrum of media has been difficult. But, rhetorical scholars have been and will be very busy with this—this is not the moment for disciplinary modesty. So I am grateful, in a very real way, to be forced to grapple with these ideas and to be in conversation with very smart others about them. I invite all of us to continue that work.

I am currently working on a proposal for a book project on conservative rhetorical style. In that proposal, I am thinking through features of conservative style like the obsession with footnotes in popular press conservative books—footnotes that give a veneer or gloss of legitimate scholarly research to an opinion industry comprised largely of recycled backwash and the hauntings by the ghosts of Goldwater and Reagan. "Epistemic closure" is a term popularized by Cato Institute fellow Julian Sanchez in his description of the fragility of the conservative media ecosystem. Immediately following David Frum's ouster from the American Enterprise Institute for having written that Obamacare would be the GOP's "Waterloo," Sanchez writes, "Reality is defined by a multimedia array of interconnected and cross promoting conservative blogs, radio programs, magazines, and of course, Fox News. Whatever conflicts with that reality can be dismissed out of hand because it comes from the liberal media, and is therefore ipso facto not to be trusted."[1]

The book also looks at victimhood. In the middle to late part of the 20th century, Kenneth Burke theorized what he calls the guilt-purification-redemption cycle, something of an update of the idea of Hebrew prophecy. Biblical prophets were burdened with a call to blast their own communities as sinners against God, to entreat them to repent, and to offer a path to redemption and a new covenant with God if they stop sinning. But of course, we do not stop sinning. So in Burke's formulation, we sin against a belief or set of values (for instance, a conservative who voted for Obama—a sin against the "tribe"), and our sin creates feelings of guilt. We are motivated to purge or purify ourselves of that guilt and that can be done in two ways: scapegoating or mortification. In scapegoating, we point to some third party to act as the "victim" in our purification ritual. For eight years, Barack Obama served as perhaps the single greatest conservative scapegoat for any and all "ills." He was the victim they would sacrifice again and again to purge their feelings of guilt. The other avenue to purify yourself of guilt upon sinning is mortification, or self-blame. We very rarely see this kind of purification ritual because, frankly, most people do not want to take it, nor do they feel they bear responsibility for society's sins. A notable recent example of mortification, however, is Arizona Senator Jeff Flake's book, *The Conscience of a Conservative*, in which he muses:

> Too often, we observe the unfolding drama along with the rest of the country, passively, all but saying, *"Someone should do something!"* without seeming to realize that that someone is us. And so, that unnerving silence in the face of an erratic executive branch is an abdication, and those in positions of leadership bear particular responsibility.[2]

If we successfully purge our sin through these victimage rituals (either scapegoating or mortification), we are redeemed. The problem is, the cycle just starts right up again because we just keep sinning. One of the consistent features of conservative rhetoric generally, and Trump's rhetoric particularly, is that guilt is purged through scapegoating usually a strawperson (extreme caricature) or imagined other—Barack Obama, Hillary Clinton, people of color, the poor, women, and so on.

And finally, conservative rhetoric tends to be apocalyptic. That is, it sets up a set of grievances such that conservatives are constantly outraged, and then uses that outrage to channel action against "sinners" like feminists or liberals or Democrats. It does not particularly matter that many of these grievances are manufactured or blown massively out of proportion so long as it produces an us-versus-them siege mentality among conservative media audiences. And I think a good case could be made that Trump's rhetoric is characterized by all of these features—a desire to sound smarter than he is, a quick temper when challenged, a constant scapegoating of some imagined other, and a sense the world is ending because of immigration or feminism or NFL players kneeling. His slipperiness as a rhetor makes him difficult to pin down and makes a cogent strategy of response even more challenging.

In this chapter, though, I would like to focus on populism. I am most certainly not the first to call Trump a populist, though I think it is one moniker of many that fit. What I would like to do is to call attention to how Trump's populist style connected and connects with a subset of voters and citizens. I argue style is a logos or a logic. Each of us puts together a style that gets "read" by others as successful or unsuccessful for the communities of which we are a part. I live in the Pacific Northwest in the epicenter of hipsterdom, for instance. Wearing a handlebar mustache, manicured flannel shirt, being heavily inked, working as a tech-bro, riding a longboard, listening to Band of Horses, complaining about traffic, driving a Tesla, and skipping work to "shred the gnar" are all main-stream for people from this region of a particular social class.

But take this brand of hipster tech-bro and put him in Macon, Georgia and his style is not likely to resonate or read well. This logic is what Pierre Bourdieu would call a "habitus," an ingrained set of habits, largely based on our life experiences, that we perform publicly.[3] Those "habits" or "logics" are physiological (an accent, slang, dress, and so on), psychological (a kind of consistency of a person's identity that makes that person recognizable), and sociological (done publicly). I'll start with scholarly literature on populism and some insight into the worldview and values of Trump voters. But I will spend most of my time unpacking how Trump's populist style is performed, mediated, received, and circulated as a set of aesthetic practices that construct Trump, for some, as the champion of "the people," the savior who will deliver us from the last eight years of godlessness, brown people, and federal overreach. Ultimately, I argue that the danger in Trump's populist style is not populism itself, but his ability to use populist rhetorical appeals as a legitimizing and galvanizing mechanism for xenophobia, ethnocentrism, and white nationalism.

Populism

Populism is, fundamentally, a rhetorical claim of representation, a reference to an imagined community of "the people."[4] "The people" may be constituted in any number of ways, but the most common in populism are: (1) the people as a nation (nationalism is particularly common in right-wing populism), (2) the people as a social class (this sort of Marxist/materialist take on community is common in left-wing populism), and (3) the people as politically sovereign (the people as "agents" is common in populism in democratic states). In other words, populism is not necessarily a conservative form of politics or rhetoric, but it can be.

Trump's populism is based on an ethno-nationalist foundation, a key danger in right-wing populism. While it is instructive to understand what populism is, it is more significant for this chapter to look at what populists do in their rhetorical appeals. Three central tropes emerge in the literature. First, populism is about "the people" — populist rhetors stress a sense of community, and, particularly, a kind of "ideal" community of people in "the heartland." This is not necessarily a rural righteousness claim (though it can be), but it certainly demarcates "patriots" from "traitors" and "real citizens" from "fake" ones.

If we consider how often media outlets have asked urban dwellers and elites to try to understand the wants, needs, and motivations of Trump voters, then we are familiar with the populist nod to "real Americans" — hint: if you are reading this book, you probably are not one. Indeed, if you are an urban dwelling elite, this kind of populism suggests you are not, and never will be, a "real American." Second, populism creates an antagonism with an Other. Like Burke's guilt-purification-redemption cycle, in which a set of agreed upon Others are scapegoated to purge a community of guilt, and like apocalyptic rhetoric in which the righteous are besieged by sinners, the "Other" is central to populist rhetorics. This Other is twofold — on one level, populism's efforts to create, in this case, a profile of Trump voters as "real Americans" points to non-Trump citizens as somehow not "real Americans." The Other, on this level then, is/are racial and ethnic minorities, undocumented persons, LGBTQ persons, coastal liberals, and so on. A second Other is political elites — "the people" have had enough of the abuse of power that seeks to marginalize and disempower them.

Third and finally, populism requires a constant perception of crisis. It is important to note these crises need not be real so long as "the people" believe they are. This anomie fuels a strong sense of identification with "the people" and simultaneously, a growing animosity toward the Other. In other words, crisis is not a bug for populism but a feature because it enables an "us versus them" siege mentality. The Other is, of course, to blame for these crises. We see how these three tropes are integrated in populist discourse generally and Trump's populism particularly.

Trump Voters

To understand Trump's rhetorical appeals, we need to get more familiar with the audiences for whom Trump's specific populist style resonates. Because populist rhetorics tend to invoke economic motivations, much was made during and after the election about the supposed economic anxiety that drove voters in the Rust Belt, Coal Country, and rural America to Trump. The Brookings Institute notes that while only 472 counties in the United States voted for Hillary Clinton (though she won by nearly 3 million votes), the counties she carried represent 70% of the entire country's economic activity. Clinton counties are the more populous, more educated, more prosperous parts of this country. So while 2584 counties carried Donald Trump to an Electoral College victory, those counties are far more likely to be economically disadvantaged.[5] It would make sense, then, that the economy might be a major driver in this election. Blog entries and think pieces and journalistic opinion following the election consistently amplified the role that economic anxiety played in electing Trump president.

And yet we know from survey data that racial resentment was significantly more likely to predict Trump voter support than economic anxiety. More specifically, fear of an increasing racial diversity in this country was the primary driver of Trump support. Notably, this fear centers on non-white immigrants and the perception that Black Americans are increasingly influential in politics and culture. On average, white people are less optimistic about rising diversity in this country than are people of color. Republicans and voters with a high school diploma or less have the most negative views of racial diversity. Indeed, *reminding* whites with strong racial identifications that racial diversity is increasing in this country makes those voters more likely to view Trump favorably. Controlling for age, race, income, party identification, and gender, models find that negative views on rising diversity predict support for Trump, but did not predict prior support for either McCain or Romney — these views are discretely true for Trump support, even among Republicans. In addition, vote switching from Obama in 2012 to Trump in 2016 is correlated with a negative view of diversity and a fear of immigration.[6]

Rhetorical Style

I talk about Trump's populism in terms of style because of style's extraordinary ubiquity, an "unprecedented investment in the aesthetic."[7] In other words, we live in a moment in which politics is highly aesthetic and stylized—we follow what politicians are wearing, what social media they use, their slogans and catchphrases, their lifestyles, but may know very little about their actual policy preferences or voting records. For instance, early in his presidency, Obama ordered a hamburger with Dijon mustard, and Sean Hannity splashed "PRESIDENT POUPON" across the screen on his show that night to castigate Obama for liking "foreign mustard" on his burger. Dijon is elitist, foreign, and possibly Kenyan—"real Americans" eat ketchup made in the U-S-of-A. A highly aestheticized politics means that even what Obama puts on his burger has political meaning.

Stuart Ewen remarks that style can be found "on news magazines, sports magazines, music oriented magazines, magazines about fashion, architecture and interior design, automobiles, and sex" and that style, therefore, becomes a "key to understanding the contours of contemporary culture."[8] If style is everywhere, then our social and political experiences are stylized. Rhetoric and public culture scholar Robert Hariman explains that as "relations of control and autonomy are negotiated through the artful composition of speech, gesture, ornament, décor, and any other means for modulating perception and shaping response," literally, our world "is *styled*."[9] Style, then, is not a method for cataloguing, but a vehicle for "understanding the dynamics of our social experience or the relationship between rhetorical appeals and political decisions."[10] In other words, we make sense of the world through style. If you present yourself as a Seattle-variety hipster tech-bro, I am going to make political inferences about you from your style.

Style and aesthetics are everywhere, "a preoccupation of nearly all sectors of society."[11] Sociologist Michael Maffesoli explains that style "becomes an all-encompassing form, a 'forming form' that gives birth to whole manners of being, to customs, representations, and the various fashions by which life in society is expressed."[12] Barry Brummett, who studies rhetorical style, echoes Maffesoli in positioning style as central when he writes, "Style... is the transcendent ground in which the social is formed in late capitalism," the "global terrain of shared knowledge, action and judgment."[13] In other words, from food to home décor, runway shows to reality television, politics to religion, and everywhere in between, style dominates the 21st century as a vehicle for making and understanding meaning. And importantly for this chapter, our politics are styled.

I have posited elsewhere that style is a logos — a logic put together by an individual to be read and judged as favorable by a community. A person's physiological choices like clothing and posture, psychological choices like consistency around a particular identity, and sociological choices like the communities in which that person moves are all part of that person's style. I have a number of friends, for instance, who have gotten into ultra-marathons and triathlons. In conversations in person and on social media sites, these friends will use a vernacular associated with intense athletic competitions. They talk about their "long run," how they are "tapering" prior to event day, and where they bought their "tri kit." They post pictures of themselves before, during, and after races. They talk about the difficulty of mentally gearing up for something like a 50-mile run. They talk to other distance runners and triathletes and exchange tips, or tell war stories. And they subscribe to *Runner's World,* read triathlon blogs like Slowtwitch.com, shop at local specialty stores, and so on. These friends, like all people, are bricoleurs (someone who cobbles different things together) of "endurance athlete style." Their decisions about how they speak, how they define themselves, and how they circulate this narrative about themselves are stylistic ones, aesthetic ones. Like all styles, "endurance athlete style" pulls together elements from a "symbolic repertoire but organizes them in a limited, customary set of communicative designs."[14] That is, people put different brands, language choices, and other symbols together to communicate who they are and what they value—their style.

Like runners, the way we see and move through the world, and the ways in which we enact our politics are defined largely by aesthetics. Perhaps no politician is more committed to or shaped by aesthetic than Trump. Trump, like most populists, began his campaign by constructing an in-group of patriots— this is an esoteric claim of membership among the chosen or faithful. We can think of myriad examples of Trump's in-group construction as a populist stylist, but one that jumps out is Stanford University's symbol of the year: the Make America Great Again red hat. The ball cap (made in *GIIINNNNAAAA*) was everywhere during the campaign. It has a kind of Ashton Kutcher-esque, ironic trucker hat feel, like the wearer can afford to spend $30 on a something that looks like it comes from the corner gas station in order to appear as if he is connecting with "the people." The hat is a visible marker of in-group member-ship. It has his slogan, "Make America Great Again," in white, block lettering. It is bright red, a common color in political campaigning. And like other aesthetic choices, it has social cache with a certain audience. That is, no one buys the MAGA hat solely for its use value.

The hat may be useful—it might keep your head warm or your hair controlled—but people wear the hat because it has exchange value. Said differently, the MAGA hat carries cultural meanings—the Trump "brand" transfers to the wearer. As Barry Brummett contends, "exchange value forms a kind of economy of its own"[15] in that "the cultural realm... has its own logic and currency."[16] Just as my friends wear the "right" brands of shoes or wetsuits, ride the "best" tri bike, and read the "right" literature to present a cohesive identity as an endurance athlete, MAGA hat-wearers don this accessory not because they need a hat, but because they want to communicate an identity by wearing *this hat*. Of course, there are people who interact with endurance athletes and enthusiastically engage on topics like carb loading and speed training, and then there are people who are tired of listening to people blather about their hobby. That is, some audiences are going to read "endurance athlete style" as resonant and others will not. The same goes for MAGA hat wearers—the hat resonates with the "right" audiences of "patriots" and "real Americans."

If we take the MAGA slogan and connect it to data on Trump voter motivations and attitudes, we might wonder: for whom is Trump making America great again? He promised again and again to bring back coal and manufacturing,[17] to build a wall on our southern border,[18] to deport undocumented people,[19] to ban Muslims from entering the country.[20] This construction of Trump's in-group offers his voters a return to an America when white men's rule was preordained, unquestioned, unchallenged—or MORE preordained, unquestioned, unchallenged. When women and people of color and LGBTQ people knew their places. We see this same kind of rhetorical construction of "the people" across Trump's campaign. Implicitly and explicitly, Trump speaks to the white working class, white people without college degrees, practicing Christians. Or as Willie Robertson of "Duck Dynasty" fame said at the Republican National Convention, Trump understands "regular folks like us who like to hunt and fish and pray and actually work for a living... people from middle America." On March 5, 2017, Trump tweeted, "Thank you for the great rallies all across the country. Tremendous support. Make America Great Again!"[21] And on February 25, 2017, he tweeted, "Maybe the millions of people who voted to MAKE AMERICA GREAT AGAIN should have their own rally. It would be the biggest of them all!"[22]

Not only does Trump stylistically construct an in-group, but in constructing this ideal American, he positions everyone else as "Other." In his 2nd debate against Hillary Clinton, he referred to her as "that nasty woman" and to Mexican men crossing into this country as "bad hombres." In a February 21, 2017 tweet, Trump announced, "The so-called angry crowds in home districts of some Republicans are actually, in numerous cases, planned out by liberal activists. Sad!"[23] And on February 23rd, he stated, "Seven people shot and killed yesterday in Chicago. What is going on there—totally out of control. Chicago needs help!"[24]

But it is not just feminists or people of color, it is also institutions that are "Other" and deserve scorn. As he tweets on February 24, "FAKE NEWS media knowingly doesn't tell the truth. A great danger to our country. The failing @nytimes has become a joke. Likewise @CNN. Sad!"[25] And, of course, excluding Trump, our corrupt politicians and political system as highlighted in his February 26th tweet, "The race for DNC Chairman was, of course, totally 'rigged.' Bernie's guy, like Bernie himself, never had a chance. Clinton demanded Perez!"[26] As in Burke's guilt-purification-redemption cycle, Trump's populist style enacts "purifies" Trump supporters by scapegoating a series of easily traced groups (people of color, women, immigrants, and so on) and institutions ("fake media" in general and the *New York Times* in particular, military, the United Nations, etc.).

Perhaps nothing more stylistically exemplifies Trump's populism than his rallies. To have style that resonates, a person needs to project a certain persona and that persona needs to remain fairly consistent. And while we should be talking about Trump's near-total lack of consistency in political positions, his projected identity is easily traced over decades and relatively stable. For a man who stated in a court deposition that his net worth is what he feels it is on any given day,[27] for a man who marks everything he can with his name, *feeling adored and admired* are fundamental to Trump's emotional state. Rallies, then, serve two purposes. The first purpose is personal for Trump—even as his overall approval ratings slide to the lowest numbers ever recorded at this point in any presidential term, rallies serve as a way to boost his energy and mood.[28]

Beyond armchair psychologizing, though, Trump's rallies serve a distinctive rhetorical function deeply connected to an aestheticized politics. Trump's rallies are a performance of a worldview and an identity — that is, a performance of his style. As psychologists Stephen Reicher and Alexander Haslam argue, "A Trump rally was a dramatic enactment of a specific vision of America. It enacted how Trump and his followers would like America to be. In a phrase, it was an identity festival that embodied a politics of hope."[29] These rallies are long. They are designed to have continual build-up through music, entertainment, and opening speakers. That build-up leads to Trump, the adored rock star, speaking "from the heart."

He may have prepared remarks, but he veers off them notably and consistently to speak off the cuff. He pauses for cheering. He spouts catch phrases. Rallies are freewheeling, not stodgy. Trump has the freedom to do and say whatever he wants. These are his people. He is unabashedly male, rich, and white, and he lets his confederates know they should not have to contend with having their own "authority" as white people or as men questioned.

Implicit in these rallies is that ever-present undercurrent of ethno and white nationalism, sprinkled with a dash of misogyny for good measure. Here, braggadocio and mockery are welcome features, a show of strength. And like the MAGA red hat, these rallies are not for everyone. Some look at these rallies and see and hear echoes of other demagogic leaders and incitement to violence.[30] Others, though, see America as they remember it or as they wish it to be. Trump does not do press conferences often and he clearly feels defensive in traditional, organized political situations. Rallies, though, enable his aesthetic identity to be nurtured, sustained, and projected.

And finally, an important function of his style is that Trump creates the perception of a constant and never-ending stream of crises (again, apocalyptic rhetoric). These crises serve to galvanize and organize his in-group against his out-group. For instance, on February 26th, Trump tweeted, "Russia talk is FAKE NEWS put out by the Dems, and played up by the media, in order to mask the big election defeat and the illegal leaks!"[31] On March 2nd, he tweeted, "The Democrats are over-playing their hand. They lost the election, and now they have lost their grip on reality. The real story is all of the illegal leaks of classified and other information. It is a total 'witch hunt!'"[32] And of course, who can forget his March 4th tweet series in which he announces, "Terrible! Just found out that Obama had my 'wires tapped' in Trump Tower just before the victory. Nothing found. This is McCarthyism!"[33] and "How low has President Obama gone to tapp [sic] my phones during the very sacred election process. This is Nixon/Watergate. Bad (or sick) guy!"[34]

Trump's obsessive use of Twitter is well established. Equally well established is his campaign operatives' and current aides' efforts to keep Trump away from both Twitter and cable television news such that he cannot fly off the handle in public tantrums.[35] But in the same way that television as a medium will forever be linked to bringing Richard Nixon and John F. Kennedy into Americans' living rooms, Twitter is inextricably connected to Trump both as candidate and as president. His Twitter posts range from platitudes about America to complaints about particular public figures to threats against other countries. Trump views Twitter as his medium to speak directly to the American people.[36] He also understands his tweets garner considerable attention and circulation. For a person who considers ratings the coin of the realm, Twitter makes sense for Trump's populist style.

Significantly, much of Trump's populist rhetorical perform-ance plays out in highly mediated ways—that is, televised speeches or, more famously, on Twitter. What Trump lacks in coherent political philosophy or policy, he makes up for in aesthetic and stylistic performance, mediation, and circulation. His creation of an in-group that is implicitly and explicitly white, Christian, native-born, and overwhelmingly male, his denigration of an out-group comprised of people of color and women who vote for Democrats and coddle violent immi-grants, and his manufactured outrage on a series of perceived

crises[37] construct an image of Trump as a man of "the people,"
a champion against the perceived threat of the Other, and the
sole arbiter of justice in the midst of profound crisis. All topped
with a poorly made but expensive ball cap.

All of these aesthetic choices are put together in Trump's
populist style, in part and in total as a cover for white
nationalism. Even before Steve Bannon's appointment or Jeff
Session's confirmation or the executive orders banning travel
from seven predominantly Muslim nations or Trump's
criticism of NFL players kneeling to criticize police brutality
against black and brown people, Trump's populist style offered
his beliefs and his followers cover for white nationalism—his
stylistic bombast, speaking off the cuff, channeling the "every
man," speaking from the gut—all of these features enabled a
performance of a sort of parrhēsiastes, someone speaking difficult truths to power.

And these truths are those that his in-group understands
because they are chosen to receive this wisdom—walls on our
southern border are important because of "bad hombres" and
rapists. Chicago's crime is an obsession because it is predominantly non-white, even though other cities, like St. Louis,
that voted overwhelmingly for Trump have more gun violence
and violent crime than Chicago, but are "his people." There has
been a tremendous rise in antisemitism and threats to and
violence against synagogues, a rise in Islamophobia and threats
to and violence against mosques, and a rise in threats to and
violence against people of color, people with "Arab" sounding
names, people traveling from countries where populations are
largely non-white.

Populism can exist in other places on the political spectrum
—we see the strength of an economic populism that Bernie
Sanders champions. But with Trump, populism is overwhelmingly about brown and black and non-Christian and women
and gay people enacting crime and taking your jobs and dis-
respecting our values and ruining America. Trump's voters
know what makes America great, and diversity, tolerance, and
your hippie bullshit certainly are not it. And while we can

speak about his populism as a way to gloss misogyny and other prejudices, overwhelmingly his performance, mediation, and circulation serve to reinforce whiteness and to demonize non-white persons through aspersions cast on race, ethnicity, nationality, and religion.

I think the natural question is, then, "what do we do about it?" Trump's populist style is already showing pronounced signs of weakness in terms of broader appeal, and we should examine reasons why that might be. It may be that people like tradition more than they realized they did — norm violation and "shaking things up" are more effective rhetorical strategies for campaigning than for governance. Conservatives like Evan McMullin, Bill Kristol, and David Frum argue that populism is not a governing philosophy. I am not sure I would stake a lot of money on that claim — I think populism could be a governing philosophy if it is attached to an actual set of policies. Trump's populist style, though, is not tethered to an actionable set of political values or initiatives. Trump's style made his followers feel affirmed. During the campaign, his slipperiness was useful — he could stand for anything, really, because he stood for nothing. But ultimately, even his followers expect him to accomplish something. If he responds solely with rallies and tweets, it becomes more difficult for his style to resonate. Ultimately, a consistent psychological style (in the Bourdieu habitus sense) requires identity to be attached to a stable center. If, as Dorothy Parker famously said about Oakland, there is no "there there," a style loses efficacy and persuasiveness.

Regardless, the damage Trump's populist style has caused and continues to cause is very real. His comments that neo-Nazi and white supremacist groups marching on the University of Virginia's campus have some "good people" in them, his description of NFL players following Colin Kaepernick's lead and taking a knee to protest police brutality as "sons of bitches," and his unwillingness to condemn even egregious acts of white terror and violence have all contributed to a kind of cultural and social toxicity. In this anomie, Very Serious People defend Robert E. Lee as an honorable man. Whether they are conscious of it or not, their attempt to maintain Con-federate statues is a stylistic reminder of white power. The xenophobia and ethno-nationalism that rallied and rallies his base has exposed a huge segment of the American populace as both inheriting and celebrating a legacy of white supremacy, homophobia, and misogyny that many thought we tran-scended during the relatively stable eight years of Obama. America is not post-anything; we are all products of this toxic bloodline. And Trump has given that movement's most vocal advocates a platform and a microphone, a hat, a rally, a slogan, and a social medium—a style—designed to amplify their worldview. While we may feel good that Trump's populist style is experiencing setbacks, we must also be vigilant to the extraordinary danger it poses for democratic institutions and public deliberation.

Notes

[1] Julian Sanchez, "Frum, Cocktail Parties & the Threat of Doubt," *JulianSanchez.com*, March 26, 2010, http://www.juliansanchez.com/2010/03/26/frum-cocktail-parties-and-the-threat-of-doubt/.

[2] Jeff Flake, "My Party Is in Denial About Donald Trump," *Politico*, July 31, 2017, http://www.politico.com/magazine/story/2017/07/31/my-party-is-in-denial-about-donald-trump-215442.

[3] Pierre Bourdieu, *Distinction: A Social Critique of the Judgement of Taste* (Cambridge: Harvard University Press, 1984), 56.

[4] Ruth Wodak & Michael Krzyzanowski, *Qualitative Discourse Analysis in the Social Sciences* (New York: Palgrave McMillan, 2008), 103.

[5] Mark Muro and Sifan Liu, "Another Clinton-Trump Divide: High-Output America versus Low-Output America," *Brookings Institute*, November 29, 2016, https://www.brookings.edu/blog/the-avenue/2016/11/29/another-clinton-trump-divide-high-output-america-vs-low-output-america/.

[6] Sean McElwee and Jason McDaniel, "Economic Anxiety Didn't Make People Vote for Trump, Racism Did," *The Nation*, May 8, 2017, https://www.thenation.com/article/economic-anxiety-didnt-make-people-vote-trump-racism-did/.

[7] Stuart Ewen, *All Consuming Images: The Politics of Style in Contemporary Culture* (New York: Basic Books, 1990), 235.

[8] Ewen, *All Consuming Images*, 2.

[9] Robert Hariman, *Political Style: The Artistry of Power* (Chicago: University of Chicago Press, 1995), 2–3.

10 Hariman, *Political Style*, 8.
11 Ewen, *All Consuming Images*, 3.
12 Michael Maffesoli, *The Contemplation of the World: Figures of Community Style* (Minneapolis: University of Minnesota Press, 1996), 5.
13 Barry Brummett, *A Rhetoric of Style* (Carbondale: Southern Illinois University Press, 2008), 3.
14 Hariman, *Political Style*, 11–12.
15 Brummett, *A Rhetoric of Style*, 14.
16 Mike Featherstone, *Consumer Culture and Postmodernism* (New York: Sage, 1991), 89.
17 Michael Bloomberg, "Trump's Promise to Bring Back Coal Jobs is Worse than a Con," *Washington Post*, May 2, 2017, https://www.washingtonpost.com/opinions/trumps-promise-to-bring-back-coal-jobs-is-worse-than-a-con/2017/05/02/8aecd0b4-2e91-11e7-8674-437ddb6e813e_story.html?utm_term=.4cce0968b03b.
18 Mike Memoli, "Despite Trump Promises, There are Still No Plans for a Mexican Border Wall," *NBC News*, September 14, 2017, https://www.nbcnews.com/politics/immigration/despite-trump-promises-there-are-still-no-plans-mexican-border-n801361.
19 Teresa Puente, "The Nightmare of Donald Trump's Deportation Promise," *TIME*, November 10, 2016, http://time.com/4566512/donald-trump-deportation-promise/.
20 Mallory Shellbourne, "Trump Call for Muslim Ban Deleted from Site After Reporter's Question," *The Hill*, May 8, 2017, http://thehill.com/homenews/administration/332404-trump-call-for-muslim-ban-deleted-from-campaign-site-after-reporters.
21 Donald J. Trump, Twitter post, March 5, 2017, https://twitter.com/realdonaldtrump/status/838441522546769923?lang=en.
22 Donald J. Trump, Twitter post, February 25, 2017, https://twitter.com/realdonaldtrump/status/835465719970217984?lang=en.
23 Donald J. Trump, Twitter post, February 21, 2017, https://twitter.com/realdonaldtrump/status/834181712783560705?lang=en.
24 Donald J. Trump, Twitter post, February 23, 2017, https://twitter.com/realdonaldtrump/status/834916167177371648?lang=en.
25 Donald J. Trump, Twitter post, February 24, 2017, https://twitter.com/realdonaldtrump/status/835325771858251776?lang=en.
26 Donald J. Trump, Twitter post, February 26, 2017, https://twitter.com/realdonaldtrump/status/835814988686233601?lang=en.
27 Kiran Khalid, "Trump: I'm Worth Whatever I Feel," *CNN.com*, April 21, 2011, http://money.cnn.com/2011/04/21/news/companies/donald_trump/index.htm.
28 David Smith, "Why Trump Still Needs the Roar of the Crowd," *The Guardian*, August 6, 2017, https://www.theguardian.com/us-news/2017/aug/05/donald-trump-rallies-supporters-west-virginia.
29 Stephen Reicher and Alexander Haslam, "Trump's Appeal: What

Psychology Tells Us," *Scientific American*, March 1, 2017, https://www.scientificamerican.com/article/trump-rsquo-s-appeal-what-psychology-tells-us/.

30 Ainara Tiefenthaler, "Trump's History of Encouraging Violence," *New York Times*, March 14, 2016, https://www.nytimes.com/video/us/100000004269364/trump-and-violence.html.

31 Donald J. Trump, Twitter post, February 26, 2017, https://twitter.com/realdonaldtrump/status/835916511944523777?lang=en.

32 Donald J. Trump, Twitter post, March 2, 2017, https://twitter.com/realdonaldtrump/status/837491607171629057?lang=en.

33 Donald J. Trump, Twitter post, March 4, 2017, https://twitter.com/realdonaldtrump/status/837989835818287106?lang=en.

34 Donald J. Trump, Twitter post, March 4, 2017, https://twitter.com/realdonaldtrump/status/837996746236182529?lang=en.

35 Clark Mindock, "Donald Trump's Aides 'Trying to Keep Him Off Twitter and Away from TV During Comey Testimony," *The Independent*, June 8, 2017, http://www.independent.co.uk/News/world/americas/us-politics/trump-comey-testimony-latest-twitter-tv-away-tweeting-white-house-aides-latest-a7779636.html.

36 Kenneth Walsh, "Trump Uses Twitter as a Strategic Weapon," *US News & World Report*, January 6, 2017, https://www.usnews.com/news/ken-walshs-washington/articles/2017-01-06/trump-uses-twitter-as-strategic-weapon.

37 Of course, there really is a series of crises, but the crises that the out-group understands are at odds with the crises that the in-group believes are true.

Jennifer Wingard

Trump's Not Just One Bad Apple: He's the Product of a Spoiled Bunch

There has been much discussion about Donald Trump's rhetoric since he began his campaign for president in June 2015. Most of the focus has been on his vitriolic tweets and rallies against women, Muslims, immigrants, people of the Jewish faith, the LGBTQ community, as well as his political opponents. Donald Trump's tweets gained so much attention during his campaign that on October 23, 2016, *The New York Times* published a two-page spread listing "The 281 People, Places, and Things Donald Trump Has Insulted on the Campaign Trail."[1]

In addition to calling several well-respected media outlets (*The New York Times*, NBC News, *The Washington Post*, *The Associated Press*, and especially CNN) "fake news," "dishonest," and "liars," Trump also attacked many of his political adversaries, consistently calling Hillary Clinton "Crooked Hillary," Elizabeth Warren "Goofy" or "Pocahontas," and Jeb Bush "low energy Jeb." But the tweets that attracted, and still attract, the most attention are the ones where Trump uses slurs to identify particular groups (e.g. immigrants, Muslims, or women).

For example, on August 10, 2015, barely a month after making a splash announcing his presidential candidacy with a speech that named Mexican immigrants "murderers and rapists," Trump tweeted: "We must stop the crime and killing machine that is illegal immigration. Rampant problems will only get worse. Take back our country!"[2] This tweet echoes his rallying cry that immigrants are killers and solidifies his brand of shocking rhetoric, which works to identify particular groups as threats in the name of "Making America Great Again."

Although videos of crowds at his rallies chanting "Build That Wall" were central to the media's coverage of Trump's campaign, Trump's exclusionary rhetoric didn't focus exclusively on immigration. Trump also targeted people of the Muslim faith, regardless of their citizenship status. And on November 15, 2015, Trump tweeted: "The media must immediately stop calling ISIS leaders 'MASTERMINDS.' Call them instead thugs and losers. Young people must not go into ISIS!"[3] His naming of terrorists as thugs and losers echoed many of his campaign rallies wherein he implicated all people of Muslim faith as potential terrorists who may be asked to register with the government if he was elected president. We have yet to see this registry take form, but Trump's conflation of Muslims with terrorists, and name-calling terrorists as losers, has been noted as highly unusual and even shocking rhetoric for a presidential candidate.

Once Trump was elected and sworn in as President of the United States of America, the expectation was that his vitriolic, shocking rhetoric would subside or at least be tempered ("the pivot"), leaving the day-to-day routine of partisan politics to reassert itself as the status quo. And with the exception of Trump's middle-of-the-night tweets, where he defends himself and his administration against perceived attacks—tweets that are often contradicted or deleted come morning—Trump's tweets and speeches have been somewhat attenuated to sound more presidential. However, the core need to define "America" through exclusion is still central to Trump's rhetoric. And because of his commitment to defining those who are threats to the US very publicly, each day under the Trump presidency has been shocking, and even a bit unsettling.

Whether one is a critic or a supporter of Trump's "shocking" behavior, one thing is clear: he is not behaving in a typically presidential manner. Instead, he seems to be playing by new rules for the leader of the free world. Trump's rules tend to disavow etiquette, tradition, and polish. For instance, one of Trump's clearest campaign promises was to "drain the swamp," or simplify the inner workings of government by removing bureaucracy and rewriting policy in simpler terms. And for those Americans who have felt that Washington has been a bloated, ineffectual system for far too long, Trump's promise was music to their ears. In other words, Trump's most ardent supporters are fortified by his *un*presidential behavior and by his *shocking* assertions.

Trump and Hate

But Trump didn't only campaign on the shocking promise of "draining the swamp." If he had, his election would be far more understandable to the vast majority of the US public (though probably equally as troubling to Democrats). What is far more concerning is Trump's use of vitriolic rhetoric to isolate particular, non-white, non-male populations as "problem" groups or even as existential threats to the US as a whole. Trump's campaign rallies, which he has continued holding well into his presidency, are founded on the rhetoric of "Othering"—wherein particular groups are isolated as threats or distasteful members of the larger US community.

As I have written elsewhere, the rhetorical act of using "Others" to define an ideal American citizenry works not only to solidify national borders. It also helps to ease the anxiety of American workers who have seen their jobs downsized and offshored due to international trade agreements and the easing of corporate oversight.[4] By creating a narrative of Americans versus "Others," those who feel disenfranchised can find a new version of American-ness to identify with—one that is central to the identity of the US and that must be protected from the assaults by other groups who do not belong. During his campaign, many considered the crass manner Trump adopted when he discussed minority groups to represent a "new low in political discourse." Everyone was always so *shocked*. But

Trump's logic of exclusion, in fact, functioned as it has throughout American history: to create an in-group (who may reap the
benefits of being American) and an out-group ("Others" who
threaten those benefits).

On the campaign trail we saw Trump demonize Muslims,
Latinx immigrants, LGBTQ citizens, peaceful protestors, and
women. During Trump's rallies he baits the crowd by selling
hatred against particular groups, and few of his supporters
seems to notice that these groups are often some of the most
vulnerable populations in the US. Moreover, shortly after
Trump's inauguration ceremony began, whitehouse.gov
underwent a transformation.[5] The Trump administration
removed or replaced the pages referencing LGBTQ rights, Civil
Rights, the Affordable Care Act, and Climate Change.
Additionally, they removed the option to read the entire site in
Spanish. Throughout both his campaign and administration,
Trump has continually defined "Americans" through opposition, by targeting groups who needed policing and/or
expulsion from the US.

When groups who have been targets of Trump's vitriolic
rhetoric begin to see their presence erased from federal websites, the painful process of delegitimation—of being turned
into an out-group—by the state becomes all too real. Such
changes may seem trivial, but whitehouse.gov is not merely an
informative website. It is also a representational space where
the current administration can engage with the public, sharing
its positions and other information on many important debates.
When certain groups are literally erased from the website, they
are being told that the current administration does not see their
issues as germane to the national agenda. Furthermore, the
deletion or revision of the language of pages focused on the
safety, security, and rights of a broad swath of the American
public, without a clear plan or agenda, is an indication of who
will be protected and who will not.

As president, Trump is no longer merely making *ad
hominem* attacks on minorities. Instead, he is also producing
executive orders and making judiciary appointments in

support of those biased statements. From his cabinet selections, his revolving door of press secretaries, naming Steve Bannon, the head of *Breitbart News*, as his "special advisor," and asking for high-level security clearance for his family members, Trump has demonstrated that his choices in office will not be typically presidential. These actions, together with his lack of attendance at ceremonial functions, and his late night tweeting from both his private and presidential accounts, have forwarded the idea that Trump himself is less of an "everyman's president" and more of an anti-establishment president whose main goal is to undermine the office itself. This raises the question: Is Donald Trump the nadir of political discursive practice? Is he *really* the harbinger of a new era in politics?

GOP: American through Exclusion

As I note above, Trump's use of exclusion to define a particular vision of America is not new. In fact, throughout history, minority groups (e.g. women, Native Americans, immigrants) have been targeted in order to define US citizenship through negation. And the branding of particular minority groups as threats to the nation has been a rhetorical mainstay of the Republican Party for the last several decades. The Republican Party has typically mobilized these arguments around policy at the state level. For example, California's Proposition 187 in 1994, Arizona's SB 1070 in 2010, and Alabama HB 56 in 2011 were each spurred to victory by the casting of immigrants as criminals during the respective campaigns. In all three of these instances, the GOP's rhetoric positioned the plight of the American worker and family in direct conflict with or under threat by immigrant communities. By naming immigrants as the ones who are responsible for taking our jobs and creating danger in our communities, the GOP were able to stimulate the electorate to vote for the stringent laws cited above. Trump extended this rhetoric in a stump speech prior to the election, when he stated that deporting any and all illegal immigrants would "save American lives, American jobs and American futures… together we can save America itself."[6]

Even today the debate over the threat of the "immigrant" can be seen playing out in the local and national media over the death of Kate Steinle, who was killed when a shot fired by an undocumented immigrant on Pier 14 in San Francisco ricocheted off the ground and hit Steinle.[7] The case has become a flashpoint to discuss immigration, sanctuary cities, and violence. And those with strong investments in limiting immigration have seized this case as an opportunity to demonstrate the danger of immigrants and sanctuary cities.

What happened to Steinle was a tragedy, and of course Zarate was holding the gun that went off and killed her. I am not claiming that he is completely innocent. What I am arguing is that because of its location in a high profile sanctuary city (San Francisco, CA) and Zarate's immigrant status, this particular case has been given far more media and political attention than may be warranted by the charges. In fact, Zarate was acquitted for manslaughter but was convicted of possession of a gun without a permit. Instead of discussing his case or Steinle's death as an argument for gun control, however, the media and political pundits have focused on Zarate's immigrant status and his ability to live in San Francisco without appropriate documentation. Much like the legislation passed in Arizona and Alabama, the Steinle case demonstrates that, in high profile cases especially, immigrants may readily be criminalized not first and foremost because of their actions, but rather because they are immigrants.

As in our current political moment, the criminalizing of immigration status and the exclusionary rhetorics surrounding immigration have been central to the work of the Republican Party for the past several decades. Republicans have used narratives of the "murderer and rapist" immigrant to create an image of a unified America under attack by outsiders. These narratives are not representative of the reality of immigration to America, and they have also occluded the changing demographics of Latinx immigration. Beginning in the 1980s, women — not men — were the primary immigrant population entering the US. As more and more families needed dual incomes to sustain themselves, many women from Central and South America came to the US to fill vacant domestic jobs. Moreover, immigration from other parts of the world—Asia, Africa, and Europe, especially—has accounted for an increasing proportion of immigrants. But even though the demographics were changing, the anti-immigrant rhetoric maintained that our country needed protection from the hyper-masculinized image of the male Latino criminal immigrant entering our country.

For example, in 1994 Proposition 187 was introduced in California. During this time, California was facing an economic downturn, and the text of the legislation made clear that the state needed protection from immigrants "stealing" from the state economy. It read: "The People of California find and declare as follows: That they have suffered and are suffering economic hardship caused by the presence of illegal immigrants in this state. That they have suffered and are suffering personal injury and damage caused by the criminal conduct of illegal immigrants in this state."[8] Even the legislation itself focuses on the criminality of immigrants as people unlawfully entering the state prior to noting potential criminal conduct. But in both senses, immigrants were constructed as threats to the state. And as threats from which the people of California needed protection. Again, by creating the need to exclude based on threat, US citizenship could be reified through heightened fear of Latinx immigrants.

A very similar strategy has been utilized by Trump throughout his campaign and his first 100 days in office. This is especially evident in his continued calls and executive order demanding the government "build a wall" on the US's southern border. For example, in Trump's address to the Joint Chiefs of Staff, which he tweeted key lines from on February 28, 2017, he stated: "America must put its own citizens first, because only then can we truly Make America Great Again! #JointAddress #AmericanSpirit."[9] Here we see Trump intimating that America will not be great until we focus on citizens (not immigrants). When this seemingly subtle statement is placed alongside Trump's previous campaign statements and

tweets about immigrants, illegal immigration, and the nation of
Mexico (which according to Trump's tweets is "totally
corrupt," "not our friend," and "...killing us"), Trump's
rhetoric of exclusion becomes quite clear. By highlighting the
dangerous Latinx criminals who have access to our country
through the drug trade and the threat of human trafficking,
Trump and other anti-immigrant politicians and pundits
exacerbate that image of the threatening male immigrant.

Trump's use of exclusionary rhetoric, which echoes decades
of Republican messages, helpfully demonstrates something
about his supposedly shocking rhetoric. In fact, Trump is not
an outlier, but instead is committed to the GOP's rhetoric of
exclusion and vilification of specific groups in order to solidify
an imaginary US citizenry that is under siege. Yes, Trump
makes his statements with far more flair than the typical
Republican, but as you can see from the text of Proposition 187
in 1994, the idea that US citizens need protection from criminal
Others has been circulating as a core value of the Republican
Party for many years.

Pay No Attention to the
Men Behind the Curtain

But if Trump is not an outlier, why do so many Republican
leaders treat him as one? What does the GOP have to gain by
placing an offensive president front and center in the media
cycle? As I mentioned earlier, the shock of Trump's election has
seemingly not worn off even after almost a year. Instead, it
seems that every day people turn on their phone, open their
email, or turn to social media, dreading what they might see.
"What has Trump said now?" "Did you see what he tweeted
this time?" "Have you seen the latest threat he made during X
news conference?" Even comedians, such as Patton Oswalt and
Mark Maron, have begun their standup specials commenting
on the impossibility of keeping up with the shocking stories
and statements coming from the White House.[10] The constant
state of shock caused by President Trump's speech acts and

behavior has come to be expected, but that makes the situation no less exhausting.

And it is this exhaustion that the GOP wants to foster. Let me explain: As long as Trump is dominating the media cycle with his over-the-top gaffes and insults, the public is more likely to focus their outrage on Trump's latest controversy, instead of focusing on the legislative work happening in the Republican-dominated Senate and House. In other words, Trump's excessively produced and "shocking" verbiage is a boon for lawmakers who want to radically change the policies and laws put in place over the last eight years. Trump's vitriolic, uncouth statements and behaviors draw attention, while the GOP mobilizes their conservative platform in the legislature. It turns out Trump is not so much a savvy strategist as he is an instrument that helpfully amplifies the GOP's savvy, long-standing rhetorical strategy.

Shock and Awe:
How the GOP Gets Sh%t Done

In addition to creating an image of an "American" by excluding those groups who are marked as different (e.g. Muslims, immigrants, LGBTQ, certain women), the Republicans have also discovered that it is easier to get legislation passed when the media cycle and the American public are focused on those "Others" or on various "shocking" scandals that draw our attention. In other words, the Republicans have modified the economic strategies of Milton Friedman wherein a country uses moments of war and/or natural disaster to pass through large-scale legislative and/or economic change. The fact that Trump repealed DACA (Deferred Action for Childhood Arrivals) in the midst of the recovery of Hurricane Harvey and the preparation for Hurricane Irma is not surprising. He routinely uses shocking behavior (tweets, offensive quotes, fights with foreign leaders) to distract the populace while his administration passes or repeals important legislation.

This is the tactic of shock and awe—using disaster or shock to fatigue or distract the media and the electorate so that unpopular legislation can be passed. The Trump administration has this strategy down, and his repeal of DACA is merely the most blatant example of "disaster capitalism." In *The Shock Doctrine: The Rise of Disaster Capitalism*, Naomi Klein claims that the key characteristic of the shift to free-market, laissez-faire corporatist economics is that of shock. According to Klein, Milton Friedman discovered that during times of disaster, the voting public was suitably distracted, and therefore unable to voice protest to large-scale changes.[11] Thus, the use of shock as a means to create political and economic change has been a strategy of many political parties across the globe.

If we put Trump's shocking statements and behavior in line with Friedman's edict, we begin to suspect that it is a way for the GOP to foster exhaustion, thereby capitalizing on the "shock" of Trump. The greatest irony regarding the use of shock is that when exhausted and/or traumatized by shocking events (whether they be natural disasters or manufactured political drama), the public returns to the social contract in the hopes that their civil liberties will be protected and honored by their government. Yet it is in that very moment that the government is using the public's desire for protection to erode those civil liberties and the social contract upon which they have come to rely.

Trump supporters are looking to the Republicans (and Trump) to "drain the swamp" and provide tax breaks. All the while, the appointments and tax plans coming from the Republicans are not supporting the folks in most need. Instead, the GOP is solidifying the rights and tax breaks of the 1%, and using shocking legislation and flatly false assertions about women, LGBTQ, immigrants, and Muslims to forward the legislation.

So yes, Trump *is* shocking and exhausting. And part of his appeal, not only to his staunch supporters but to the Republican Party, too, is that he is *un*presidential in everything he does. Because as long as Trump's tweets, statements, and behavior are over-the-top and sometimes offensive, he provides the shock the GOP needs to repeal eight years of democratic legislation. And as long as Trump is the one making the racist, sexist, and discriminatory statements, the GOP also have plausible deniability. You see, it is Trump, the shocking, loose-cannon president, who says those things. Ostensibly, he does not represent the core values of the Republican Party. And this leads us to the ultimate purpose of Trump as president: he is supposedly a "bad apple."

Trump as Bad Apple

So what exactly is a "bad apple"? Unlike a scapegoat, a "bad apple" is *not* a victim in the traditional sense. A "bad apple" is indeed bad—they have done bad things. They are easy to dislike or dismiss. And it is the ability to isolate and/or dismiss a "bad apple" that makes them so valuable. A "bad apple" is invoked when the media, a group, or the state needs to find an individual from within the group to take the blame for a violent or offensive event in order to maintain the status quo of the group or the state. In other words, the "bad apple" is a new form of scapegoat where individual perpetrators are used to let a larger group off the hook.

In the case of Trump, the "bad apple" works like this: As I explained earlier, the Republicans have excluded and vilified particular groups in the name of defining "American-ness" for several decades. These exclusions, however, were accomplished through scapegoating people outside of their group—through legislation and targeted state-based campaigns directed primarily against non-Republican allies.

But now, more GOP and swing voters feel disenfranchised, so the evolution of the Republican platform was to bring this exclusionary rhetoric to the national stage. But how? Unlike 2001, there was not a major security crisis like 9/11 (no shock), and unlike 2008, no large-scale economic downturn (again no shock) that the Republicans could use to help formulate these exclusions. Enter Donald Trump. Trump's unpredictable, and often offensive, rhetoric targeted the very groups who had been historically targeted by the Republicans but in a much more overt way. Trump's critics, including many of those running against him during the Republican primary, openly took issue with his rhetoric. Yet the GOP stood behind him, and his nomination. Many people have asked why.

Well, as long as it is Trump who is spouting the racist, sexist, homophobic, antisemitic, and anti-Muslim rhetoric, the GOP at large does not have to claim those sentiments as part of their platform. It does not matter that many elected GOP officials have created legislation that is equally offensive. Because Trump now speaks these shocking statements in public, the GOP can isolate those sentiments as "Trumpian" and disavow or ignore the party's involvement. "The man behind the curtain" is now at center stage.

Trump becomes the perfect "bad apple" for the GOP. It makes even more sense that Trump has become a "bad apple" when we consider the term originally gained traction in the media in response to corporate malfeasance. In their 2003 documentary, *The Corporation,* Mark Achbar and Jennifer Abbot assembled news media clips blaming corporate financial and ethical misconduct on the behavior of "a few bad apples," instead of systemic problems of corporate oversight.[12] Achbar and Abbot's focus on the language of "a few bad apples" argues that the media is complicit in protecting corporate interests by disconnecting wrongdoing from the greater corporate logics which govern our world. Instead, "a few bad apples" take the blame for the wrongdoing that is actually enabled by the legal and economic systems that allow corporations to behave "like psychopaths with no regard for others and no remorse for their harmful behavior."[13] Even "bad apple" corporations are not completely excised from corporate culture. Instead they are seen as instances of individual behavior gone awry, thus needing to be either reeducated or made of example of, but never totally expelled.

As is the case with Trump. He is never fully excised for his shocking rhetoric. Instead, he is made to be *the* face of the party, even though he is often isolated as the party's "bad apple." And in many ways, his "bad apple" behavior stimulates his base because they see him as the "bad boy" of the GOP. In other words, various Republican leaders may condemn Trump throughout his presidency, but he may never be impeached because he is so useful. Some say it is because of party loyalty, but if we consider Trump's function to the party as a "bad apple" it seems that his presidency is safe as long as he is the one who can be disavowed when he "goes too far" in saying things the Republicans want said.

Conclusion: A Year in Review

As the close of the first year of Trump's presidency nears, it becomes apparent that his time in office has not and most likely will not change Trump or his rhetoric. Many popular psychology magazines and media outlets claim that it is Trump's wealth or narcissism that will not allow for growth. And that maybe the case, but if Trump's rhetoric is put within the context of the policy and platform of the Republican Party over the last three decades, Trump becomes less of an individual anomaly and more of an outgrowth of the exclusionary rhetoric of the GOP.

But as long as Trump is presented as an anomaly, a wild card, or even crazy, the Republicans can maintain that he is indeed a "bad apple" that presents a threat to their party, too. If Trump is constructed as a "bad apple," his actions are his own, and therefore cannot be connected to larger systems that have historically followed similar patterns of oppression. In many ways, Trump becomes the savviest strategy of the GOP since "the war on terror." He says truly offensive things about minorities and vulnerable populations in an effort to define an imaginary American citizenry. The Republicans publicly denounce his rhetoric. And then they return to Congress and pass legislation that ultimately impacts the very people Trump names in his rallies and tweets as threats. And the GOP can do so with plausible deniability because, as I stated before, they get to pretend that the hate speech is "Trumpian" after all.

Notes

1   See German Lopez, "The *NY Times* Published a List of People Trump Has Insulted on Twitter. It's Quite Long," *Vox*, October 24, 2016, https://www.vox.com/policy-and-politics/2016/10/24/13387170/trump-insults-twitter. The *New York Times* list has subsequently been updated. See Jasmine C. Lee and Kevin Quealy, "The 394 People, Places and Things Donald Trump Has Insulted on Twitter: A Complete List." *New York Times*, November 17, 2017, https://www.nytimes.com/interactive/2016/01/28/upshot/donald-trump-twitter-insults.html.

2   Donald J. Trump, Twitter post, August 10, 2015, https://twitter.com/realdonaldtrump/status/630906211790102528. For more on the President's Twitter habits, see Amanda Willis and Alysa Love, "All the President's Tweets," *CNN.com*, December 12, 2017, http://www.cnn.com/interactive/2017/politics/trump-tweets/.

3   Donald J. Trump, Twitter post, November 20, 2015, https://twitter.com/realdonaldtrump/status/667686386653388800.

4   Jennifer Wingard, *Branded Bodies, Rhetoric, and the Neoliberal Nation-State* (Lantham, MD: Lexington Books, 2013).

5   The White House, "Front Page," January 22, 2017, https://www.whitehouse.gov.

6   Eric Bradner, "7 Lines That Defined Trump's Immigration Speech," *CNN.com*, September 1, 2016. http://www.cnn.com/2016/08/31/politics/donald-trump-immigration-top-lines/.

7   Phil Van Stockum, "I Saw the Kate Steinle Murder Trial Up Close. The Jury Didn't Botch It," *Politico*, December 6, 2017, https://www.politico.com/magazine/story/2017/12/06/kate-steinle-murder-trial-jury-didnt-botch-216016.

8   California State Legislature, "Proposition 187 (a.k.a The Save Our State Initiative)," *American Patrol*, June 26, 2008, http://www.americanpatrol.com/REFERENCE/prop187text.html.

9   Donald J. Trump, Twitter post, February 28, 2017, https://twitter.com/potus/status/836761614594555904.

10   Patton Oswalt, "Patton Oswalt: Annihiliation," *Netflix*, 2017; Mark Maron, "Mark Maron: Too Real," *Netflix*, 2017.

11   Naomi Klein, *The Shock Doctrine: The Rise of Disaster Capitalism* (New York: Picador, 2008).

12   Mark Achbar, Jennifer Abbot, and Joel Bakan, directors, *The Corporation* (Vancouver, BC: Big Picture Productions, 2003).

13   Achbar, Abbot, and Bakan, *The Corporation*.

Ira J. Allen

Who Owns Donald Trump's Antisemitism?

In April 2017, I attended the tail end of a so-called "Patriot's Day" in Berkeley, California.[1] It had devolved before my arrival into violent clashes between far-right militia members and antifascist counter-protesters, or so the story ran.[2] Following on two other such clashes in the preceding month and a half, rightists had flown and driven to Berkeley from all over the country to attend a "pro-Trump" rally. In internet forums, Facebook groups, and militia meetings, and with the giddiness of schoolchildren planning to play hooky, "Patriots" anticipated a rally that would be as much war as politics. On premier white supremacist website *Stormfront*, for instance, forum member LinuxGeek proclaimed, "It's about time we all start getting prepared. Come armed and move in groups. The enemy is losing the culture war. They lost control of the police force in most states and now the people are rising up."[3] Nine days later, heavily armored rightists beat black-clad antifas in the streets of Berkeley as the gathered police forces stood aside.

Unlike kids cutting school, the rightists descending on Berkeley had come, as the phrase goes, with malice aforethought. On April 15, 2017, that malice flew under white supremacist flags: rightists wearing Trump hats threw Nazi "Sieg Heil" salutes and carried signs with cryptic assertions like "Da Goyim Know" on banners bearing refashioned Nazi Ensigns composed of multiple renderings of the Trumpist meme-word "Kek."

And, of course, there was the violence itself: part of a long history of street fighting between fascists and antifascists, the ethno-nationalist right and anarchist left. In such fighting, rightists have not always mobilized under the explicit signs of antisemitism and white supremacism, but these did. Rightist "Patriots" of all descriptions marched and fought under banners explicitly devoted to antisemitism and white nationalism. Of course, as journalist Natasha Lennard noted, "This is not to say that each, or even the majority, of the hundreds of pro-Trump attendees sympathize with the Venn Diagram of white supremacist, alt-right, antisemitic, and neo-Nazi groups which intersect with the president's broader support base."[4] Rather, the point is that the constellation of hate gets interwoven at all levels *irrespective* of varying individual attitudes.

These groups end up being symbolically unified with one another—and the same goes for Trump himself, and for Trumpism broadly. This is an essay about what it means to have a *materially* antisemitic president, whether he's committed to the *ideas* of antisemitism or not.

Trumpism, Racialized Hate, and Media Legitimation

In Berkeley, not only did neo-Nazis collaborate with other, "non"-hate groups in organizing and attending the rally, but their symbols flew proudly above the rally and the clashes alike. Before, during, and after the violence, red Trump hats bobbed alongside American flags and Hitlerian emblems. Patriotism, nationalism, white nationalism, and antisemitism melded, and hardly for the first time. The #MAGA hashtag of Trump's campaign sloganeering accompanied Sieg Heil salutes in person and Twitter celebrations of the violence by "Proud Boys" identifying as "western chauvinists who refuse to apologize for creating the modern world."[5]

Celebrity white nationalist Richard Spencer took to Twitter to offer his thoughts on the violence: "Hail Victory!" (exclamation point *sic*, victory *sic*, hail *sic*).[6] The next day, antifascist organizers planned public protests against Spencer's appearance at Auburn University (initially canceled by the university and then reinstated upon Spencer's judicial appeal). Spencer retweeted the response of a fellow member of the alt-right twittersphere, a man describing himself as "Nationalist. Populist. Reactionary. #ProudGoys. #AltSouth": "The White Bloc is needed to shut down violent antifas and communists, disrupt PC on college campuses and defend free speech & assembly."[7] Against the Black Bloc, the "White Bloc."

An impatient reader might wonder, though, why we should call all this "Trump's antisemitism"? It's not like Donald Trump was out there punching antifascists in Berkeley or negotiating to get Richard Spencer a podium at Auburn. More likely, he was golfing (for personal enrichment and at great taxpayer expense[8]) at one of his own resorts. So, what's the relation?

At stake here is the public rise of antisemitism in explicit identification with the rise of Trump. This dual upsurge is accomplished through the verbal magic of what rhetorician Kenneth Burke called "consubstantiality." Consubstantiality, for Burke, was a complicated concept—it names a way of being together in language that is at once also material. It is about being "both joined and separate, at once a distinct substance and consubstantial with another."[9] It is a term for the way ideas and attitudes become substantially entwined by being placed with each other.

For instance, consubstantiality describes how flags waving together can make alliances real, alongside and regardless of the flag-wavers' explicit intentions. As Burke puts it, "in acting together, men [*sic*] have common sensations, concepts, images, ideas, attitudes that make them *consubstantial*."[10] Or, as neuroscientists say of the pathways in the brain that make us who we are, neurons that fire together wire together. There is a firing-together that twins the public shamelessness of racialized hate with Trumpism, makes them substantially one. Indeed, Trump's winning of the presidency was immediately celebrated by a wide range of antisemitic and other hate groups.[11]

Racialized hate and Trumpism are *different*, but they *are* together. And they are together through a series of symbolic identifications ranging from shared slogans to shared practices of violence.[12]

Those identifications are made possible by a media ecology that privileges outrage. Witness, for instance, the bizarre CNN chyron accompanying a segment on whether Trump should disavow Richard Spencer: "Alt-Right Founder Questions if Jews Are People." Part of what made the chyron so bizarre was that, as Sammy Nickalls put it in *Esquire*, "while Spencer is, indeed, an anti-Semite, this quote in particular was not technically about whether Jews are people. Instead, he was asking whether media figures denouncing Trump are people, or if they were soulless golems created by the Jews."[13] In other words, yes, of course, Spencer is grotesquely antisemitic. But, it is here not Spencer, but *CNN* that actually questions if Jews are people.

Still worse, CNN's ham-fisted denunciation of Spencer was accompanied by a nearly three-minute conversation about the pros and cons of denouncing white supremacists who support you.[14] The net effect was, as with much media coverage of Trumpism, to amplify antisemitism as a publicly legitimate force in American political life.

Trump's own campaign speeches and popular reception, as other contributors to this volume show, brimmed with racial and religious animus along multiple axes. He inveighed against Arabs and equated Islam with terrorism.[15] He followed long-standing Republican rhetorical policy in using lightly coded language to associate Black people with governmental waste and the unjust redistribution of resources.[16] He denigrated Latinx people, exemplified by Mexicans and presumed to be immigrants, whom he equated with violence and economic decline (both of which promised to be magically reversed by the erection of a wall).

Trump's rhetoric, as also that of his supporters, is racialized through and through, and non-whiteness is consistently identified as threatening.[17] So, it is not surprising that

Trumpism wires together with racialized hate. Nor is it especially surprising that American media outlets, hungry for clicks and eyeballs, hung on—and legitimated—his every word and those of many of his ugliest supporters. Racialized hate is a perduring strain, even a core one, of American culture and society; media systems that rely on second-by-second engagement for their existence are served equally well by giving a platform to that hate and by the outrage prompted by this platforming.

What has been more surprising, for many, has been that this toxic bloom in the rhetorical ecology of the United States has *also* included the re-licensing of antisemitism.

"But His Grandchildren Are Jewish!"

Initially, it seemed odd to associate Trump with antisemitism. After all, Trump's son-in-law, Jared Kushner, is a committed member of the religiously serious Chabad movement within Judaism and a key player in the Trump White House. Trump's daughter Ivanka converted to Judaism in 2009. Trump has long-standing ties to hardliner Israeli Prime Minister Benjamin Netanyahu, and Kushner grew up knowing the man as a family friend.[18] Trump's 2016 campaign speech to Israeli lobbying group AIPAC brought down the house with lines like, "When I become president, the days of treating Israel like a second-class citizen will end on day one"—coupled with characteristically implausible assertions such as, "[President Obama] may be the worst thing to ever happen to Israel, believe me, believe me."[19]

In Trump's proposed budget, marked by substantial cuts in US aid to all other countries, financial and military support for Israel remained untouched.[20] A heavy step further, Trump has waffled dramatically on illegal Israeli settlements in Palestinian territories, and seemed at least sometimes to be jettisoning the US's long-standing commitment to independent Palestinian and Israeli states in exchange for a single, Jewish-dominated state.[21] Indeed, Trump's chosen Ambassador to Israel, David Friedman, has a pronounced antipathy to the possibility of a

Palestinian state and deep ties to the Beit El settlement, including a house built illegally on Palestinian ground.[22]

Then, too, several of Trump's public proclamations have been either pro-Jewish or at least genuinely critical of anti-semitism. Despite badly bungling International Holocaust Remembrance Day by failing to mention Jews at all,[23] Trump pulled it together to proclaim May 2017 Jewish American Heritage Month, in accordance with a tradition begun in 2006 under President G.W. Bush. And he eventually, though reluctantly, offered a forceful condemnation of antisemitism and some indication that he would like to see it eradicated.[24]

And there remains the simple fact—again—that Trump's daughter, his son-in-law, and his grandchildren are Jewish. No US President has ever been personally closer to Jewish people. Small wonder that Jewish groups themselves have been divided over whether to identify Trump's administration with antisemitism.[25]

To the hard-eyed antisemites of *Stormfront*, all this has merited hundreds of responses to the question "Is Donald Trump another jew-puppet" (*sic*), most in the affirmative. As longtime forum member The Q wrote in early April 2017, "The Trumpfront era, the era of foolishly deluding ourselves that somehow Trump was a closet white nationalist sympathizer, is effectively over."[26] Surely, one sort of observer would con-clude, Trump is no antisemite. The loudest antisemites, at least, have come to declaim what they see as his perfidy.

Firing Together with Antisemitism

And yet, the presidential campaign, election, and early govern-ing months of Donald Trump *fired together with* antisemitic violence and threats in a manner not seen for decades.

The Anti-Defamation League (ADL) identified an astound-ing 86% increase in antisemitic incidents in the first quarter of 2017, on top of an already very worrying 34% increase through-out 2016.[27] Alarmingly, that increase has held steady, with 1,299 incidents of antisemitic assault, harassment, or vandalism through September of 2017, a total increase of 67% in the first three quarters of 2017 over the same period in 2016.[28]

During the months immediately following Trump's election, in the neighborhood of 160 Jewish community centers received bomb threats.[29] And, even before Trump officially took office, in a rash of seemingly spontaneous incidents, anti-semites painted crude swastikas on billboards, ballfield dug-outs, bus stops, and businesses nationwide. Through the 2016 campaign and the early days of Trump's presidency in 2017, Jewish cemeteries were vandalized all across the country, with hundreds of gravestones desecrated.[30] Predictably, after Charlottesville, the numbers spiked again.[31] Hate groups have begun recruiting via flyers on college campuses at a level the ADL describes as "unprecedented," with white supremacist flyering on 107 different campuses in 33 states during the 2016–17 school year.[32]

In May 2017 testimony to the Senate Judiciary Committee, ADL National Director Jonathan Greenblatt pulled no punches as he presented the link between Trumpism and antisemitism:

> The majority of anti-Semitic incidents and other hate crimes are not carried out by extremists or organized hate groups. But the extraordinarily polarizing and divisive election campaign—which featured harshly anti-Muslim rhetoric and anti-Semitic dog whistles—has coarsened the public discourse and fostered an atmosphere in which white supremacists and other antisemites and bigots feel emboldened and believe that their views are becoming more broadly acceptable. The campaign's repeated flirta-tion with these elements—retweeting their content and quoting their heroes—and the President's initial reluctance to address rising anti-Semitism, have helped to mainstream their ideas.[33]

In other words, what is at stake is a degradation of the rhetorical ecology. And Trump, as the ADL sees it, has con-tributed directly to that degradation. The resultant spike in antisemitic incidents is, in an important sense, at his doorstep.

There's no question that Trump resisted repeated calls to condemn the rise in antisemitism.[34] It wasn't that he rejected them so much as that—for whatever reason—he dodged them. For instance, when questioned in mid-February 2017 by a Hasidic member of the press corps about how he would respond to the "uptick in antisemitism" that occurred in the early days of his presidency, Trump responded with an insultingly dismissive *non sequitur*: "Sit down... I am the *least* antisemitic person that you've ever seen in your entire life."[35]

He then went on to make no pledges whatsoever to mitigate the uptick in antisemitism. Instead, his answer included the assertion that he was the "least racist person you've ever seen" and focused mostly on his own electoral success.[36] Whether intentionally or not, Trump's defensive response to this softball question, asked by a reporter from a friendly outlet, mirrored one typical response of well-established antisemites to questions about their ideology. He deflected the question of antisemitism by making and amplifying previous assertions about his character. No antisemite, and no racist, and a "huge" winner of the Electoral College to boot.

Now, it does seem unlikely that Trump is a virulent anti-semite at the level of ideas. (It is unlikely in part because that would require him to keep it a secret, and Trump seems incapable of keeping any other noxious attitudes a secret.) The thing is, interesting as it can be to try to parse and much as it makes for good copy, Trump's personal attitude only sort of matters.

On sites like *Stormfront* and subreddit /r/The_Donald, as well as face to face, antisemites initially reassured one another that "the Donald's" reticence to embrace them openly merely echoed their own approach to certain kinds of confrontation.[37] So it was that Trump's election was initially greeted by America's most virulent antisemites with sheer joy. Andrew Anglin, publisher of the influential neo-Nazi website *The Daily Stormer*, exulted on November 9, 2016: "We won, brothers... Make no mistake about it: we did this. If it were not for us, it wouldn't have been possible."[38] Before they were against him, or at least skeptical of him, neo-Nazis celebrated Trump's rise with violence and threats thereof.

If Trump is as personally close to Judaism and about as politically close to Israel as any US President has ever been, why is his political rise coupled with the rise of antisemitism, celebrated by antisemites?

If It Dodges Like an Antisemite

As should be clear by now, the picture of Trump's friendliness to Judaism is more than a little troubled. It's not that he *is* antisemitic, but that he and his followers *share a substance* with antisemitism. Moreover, Trump *habitually dodges like an anti-semite* — all the more so if you take into account his various surrogates.

Just before being punched in the head, in an interrupted interview that quickly went viral, Richard Spencer answered a question about his white supremacism by focusing on the word "neo-Nazis": "Neo-Nazis don't love me. They kinda hate me, actually."[39] Dissociating himself from neo-Nazis specifically, Spencer was sidestepping the real question about his white supremacism. The rhetorical playbook of modern white supremacists makes much of individual ideological differences, dodging direct engagement with still socially negative labels.

Trump's initial refusal to disavow the endorsement of David Duke, former Ku Klux Klan grand wizard and self-described "racial realist," is an excellent example of consub-stantiality with antisemitism. Despite a well-documented history of clear awareness of who Duke was and of his status as a Klan leader,[40] Trump's immediate response to a question about whether he would condemn Duke and white suprema-cists who endorsed his candidacy was to plead ignorance: "I don't know anything about David Duke. Okay? I don't know anything about what you're even talking about with white supremacy or white supremacists."[41]

Bizarrely, two days earlier, on February 26, 2016, Trump had already conceded, in one of the most tepid distancing moves ever undertaken by a modern political leader, "David

Duke endorsed me? Okay, all right. I disavow, okay?"[42] In other words, he unpersuasively rejected Duke before he defensively didn't know who Duke was. At such moments, Trump's personal feelings about Jews matter much less — regardless of his reasons — than his simple failure to shame antisemites at the appropriate time. He dodges like an antisemite.

And then there is Sean Spicer, a Press Secretary so incompetent he is hard to credit with genuine malice, but who contributed much to the space shared by Trumpism and anti-semitism. The list of Spicer's vaguely and less vaguely white supremacist comments was topped in April 2017 by his assertion — profoundly historically inaccurate, perhaps even intentionally antisemitic — that Syrian dictator, Bashar al-Assad, was worse than Hitler, who "didn't even sink to using chemical weapons."[43] In taking Spicer publicly to task for this and other inanities, historian Eileen Kane cogently articulates their danger:

> Many think of anti-Semitism and other forms of racism as a worldview that one deliberately embraces or rejects. But it's perhaps more useful to think of it as a creeping, infectious disease that spreads easily to people who are not particu-larly self-reflective or principled, and who understand its usefulness to their own advancement in a given context.[44]

Much antisemitism is not the antisemitism of *Stormfront* and *The Daily Stormer*. It is the indirect, but nonetheless real, anti-semitism of Sean Spicer.

American history has a long tradition of normalizing anti-semitism,[45] as in Spicer's post-Trump installment as a Fellow at the Institute of Politics in Harvard University's Kennedy School. Spicer's antisemitism is a handy attitude, a collection of implicit beliefs that are neither avowed nor disavowed, but are simply *active*. Such antisemitism is rarely punished in American life, though the rapidity of Spicer's rehabilitation after leaving the Trump White House — by scholars, no less! — should be startling.

Donald Trump's antisemitism, if conscious, likely consists in a similar low cunning, a recognition of its political usefulness. What's crucial, though, is the confluence of his (and his surrogates') symbolic actions with those of antisemites. Responding to criticism of his boss's long silence and subsequent robotic condemnation of antisemitism, Spicer complained that "no matter how many times he talks about this, it's never good enough."[46] Isn't that *just* the sort of thing a weaselly antisemite would say about a sidestepped apology or a half-hearted one given with a wink and a nod to politically expedient deplorables? With such men running the show, how could hate *not* be emboldened? And when hate is emboldened in America, it is ecumenical.

Racialized hatreds of all sorts are consubstantial with one another and with Trumpism. Antisemitism, constellated in that grim Venn diagram with other forms of racialized hate, belongs to Trump's America. This much is clear. But who, exactly, *is* Trump's America? The easy answer, one beloved of liberals both when Hillary Clinton enunciated it during the 2016 presidential campaign and still today,[47] is that it's a big basket of deplorables. But, that's too easy by half—and a pragmatically poor answer for anyone wishing to hold onto democratic hope.[48]

So, to whom, precisely, does an antisemitism that has been brought virulently back into play with Trump belong? Asking who owns Trump's antisemitism should return us to a more core political-rhetorical question: What is to be done?

Trump's America — and Ours

Antisemitism is something we all own. By that, I mean both that it is a term available to all and that it is a structural force that infuses public life in ways that are often obscure. The marking off of Jews as Other—like the marking off of Black people, Latinx people, Muslim people, GLBTQ people, trans* people, and so forth—is a rhetorical maneuver that occurs both consciously and unconsciously. It is a motion in language, and language *does not allow us to* not *mark the boundaries of community with Otherness.*

Antisemitism, as Jean-Paul Sartre argued powerfully in *Anti-Semite and Jew*, is a signal case of a general tendency. In other words, there is something in language itself that creates boundaries, walls that separate one identity from the next — and that denigrate any identity left outside those walls. At its extreme, this tendency becomes a blind, nonsensical hatred. Well before that extreme, though, it is a force in all of us (though some certainly more than others), a force that must be negotiated and cannot be simply ignored.

This essay asks what it means for a president to *have* anti-semitism without personally hating Jews (just as the same president can be a misogynist while "loving" women, a racist while claiming to love people of color, and so on[49]). At stake is a question of responsibility. To ask, "Who owns Donald Trump's antisemitism?" is also to ask "Who is responsible for the consubstantiality of antisemitism and Trumpism?"

Why have antisemitism and Trumpism risen in tandem? *How?* There are deeper rhetorical structures at play in public sentiments and action than merely the waving flags of the deplorables.

Most thoughtful people know, on at least some level, that they are implicated in the production of harmful attitudes and worldviews. We all inherit worlds of injustice that make us who and how we are, and these worlds make us to some extent in their image. It doesn't take much to see there's no way around this. But the move from that acknowledgment to a more personal sense of responsibility is hard to understand and to accept, especially if you don't *feel yourself* to be, for example, an antisemite. And doing something with that responsibility can be harder still. This is partly because our words for noxious attitudes — words like "antisemitism" — tend to operate much like the noxiously Othering words to which we object.

They coalesce into the images of Others whom We, our-selves, clearly are not. Cultural critic Chauncey DeVega puts this nicely in a 2014 primer on white supremacy, noting that "images of terrorist organizations such as the Ku Klux Klan and neo-Nazis serve as outlier caricatures of racism in the post-Civil Rights era."[50] His point is that "white racial innocence, and a sincere belief by many white folks that they do not hold racist attitudes, or benefit personally or collectively from systemic white racism, is an example of how white supremacy has evolved to make itself relatively invisible (to willfully ignorant white people) as a dominant social force in American life."[51] The personalized, reified stereotypes of *the* racist, *the* sexist, *the* antisemite habitually operate as defenses—as in Trump's response to questions about how he would address an uptick in antisemitism.

Some people, of course, *are* avowed antisemites. They fit the definition-clause that begins Sartre's *Anti-Semite and Jew*, written in the immediate aftermath of the Holocaust: "If a man attributes all or part of his own misfortunes and those of his country to the presence of Jewish elements in the community, if he proposes to remedy this state of affairs by depriving the Jews of certain of their rights... we say that he has antisemitic *opinions*." Most people in the United States are not antisemites in this sense, though some are. More generally, the percentage of avowedly antisemitic Americans has been in recent decades quite low.[52] Neo-Nazis have proliferated on Twitter and 4chan, of course, and in the Indiana and Kentucky hills. But, they knew their attitudes were unwelcome in public, unless at least semi-cloaked.

And now? As the media ecology has amplified white supremacist messages, the rhetorical landscape has grown tangled and weird. Thinking very much of Hitlerite Germany, Kenneth Burke observed of such phenomena, "[a] 'good' rhetoric neglected by the press obviously cannot be so 'communicative' as a poor rhetoric backed nationwide by headlines."[53] Even the *We* of the "resistance" in Trump's America is a national *We* that responds to headlines and chyrons that amplify and, in many cases, legitimize anti-semitism. Unreconstructed antisemites may still not be welcome in polite company, but they can now be celebrities all the same. The difficulty, however, is that They are Us.

Antisemitism, Shame, and Democratic Hope

I have rarely encountered antisemitism as a directly personalized force, one-to-one. Indirectly or passive-aggressively, however, is another matter. Particularly notable was the time a landlord accidentally forwarded correspondence with her property manager. Complaining of my intractability on some matter, she exclaimed, with the exasperation of antisemites through the ages, "Sorry he's being such a prick—Jewish boy, I'm afraid." Her property manager rose to my defense, after a fashion: "My experience with American Jews is that they're usually some of the most well-adjusted people around. Israeli Jews are a different story entirely."

In this vignette, accidentally or not so accidentally shared, the quiet antisemitism of many Americans is exposed. My landlord and her property manager were well-educated people, good liberals. The former had completed her PhD at Indiana University, where I was then studying, before she moved to a faculty position elsewhere; the latter was a well-respected member of Bloomington's broadly tolerant, open community. Though neither, I think, intended to communicate *to me* their attitudes toward Jews, they felt comfortable expressing these amongst themselves. Like most American antisemitism, theirs was not meant to be shared publicly—it was a private affair. When I confronted my then-landlord about the email by phone, she was flustered and embarrassed, ashamed even. "You have to understand," she said almost tearfully, "I'm not a *racist*."

"But I'm not a *racist*" is the rallying cry of a defense that is at once dangerous and laughable, but it is also a sign of hope. The answer is always more or less the same: Yes, you are; or we wouldn't be having this conversation. Yes, you are; you're a product of a racist system and your denial helps in its reproduction. Yes, you are; we all are, around here.[54]

At the same time, the plea opens a rhetorical possibility. My landlord didn't want to be a racist. There was room for a difficult conversation precisely *because* she felt ashamed. The appropriate response was an effort to find ways to live together well —not without anger, and not by merely pretending to tolerate each other, but in the spirit of democratic hope. That spirit eschews the urge to scapegoat. The point is not first and foremost to cast out all the antisemites, but to begin by swaying all who can be swayed. Owning and entering into conversation with our own deplorability (including the backdrop, casual antisemitism of many otherwise good liberals) is the route to a more democratic polity.

This leaves us with a different read on what presidential rhetoric is for than that typically espoused by scholars of rhetoric and politics.[55] Not merely agenda-setting or norm-defining, presidential rhetoric can be usefully expressive of what we collectively disavow. Trump's consubstantiality with antisemitism presents us with the reality of a disavowed, but no less real for that, backdrop antisemitism in American private life. Perhaps, to be effectively shamed, the darker strains of our collective pathologies must occasionally come to light. We need the figure of a grotesque Other, whom we can learn to apprehend is at once muchly Us.

In the shameful mirror of antisemitism's consubstantiality with Trumpism, much is reflected that goes far deeper than Trump. American white supremacism, before and beneath Trumpism, is an unresolved problem for democracy.

Paradoxically, presidential rhetoric can foster the conditions for democracy precisely where it is itself most anti-democratic. Harmful presidential rhetorics are consubstantial with broad swathes of the *demos* (i.e. the people at large) that reject other swathes of the *demos* as legitimate political interlocutors, and thus cannot be effectively just dismissed. Presidential rhetoric, as in the consubstantiality of Trumpism with antisemitism, marks real, existing limits of ongoing democratic polity-formation. We, accordingly, need to carefully negotiate between acceptance and repudiation in the face of "Trump's" antisemitism.

Such negotiation begins by noting but not giving undue importance to the attitudes, beliefs, and ultimately the utterances of the current White House resident. Much more, though, our job is to focus on democratic friendship where it is most difficult[56]—in feeling our way through what it means for Trump's antisemitism to exceed his own intentionality and, in some sense, to be all of ours. Only in assuming collective ownership of Trumpist antisemitism, recognizing it not as aberrant but as thoroughly American—and *also* as shameful— can we negotiate together for a more democratic polity.

There are many features of Trumpism that cry out for naming and shaming, and there are many—some, the very same—that call on us for good-willed conversation. The misogyny, the racism, the transphobia, and, yes, the anti-semitism of Donald Trump all must be publicly and vigorously resisted. And, they all must be interpersonally negotiated.

There remains a temptation to assume at the end of the day that these are ultimately just Somebody Else's problem, and that this Somebody Else is a Very Bad Person—deplorable, irredeemable—but also simply obdurately Other once words fail. There is a temptation to assume, both before and after conversation, that Somebody Else is *the whole* of the problem, that the problem is racists and antisemites and that We are not those things, and that therefore all We really need to do is more of the sorts of things that are Us, such as free speech and good-willed conversation with those who have ears to hear, and that hopefully They will just go away. This is wrong.

Burke warned against the pull to scapegoat—that is, to single out another person or group of people as "the problem" and attempt to expel them—not only because it is morally wrong, but also because it limits our democratic capabilities. Like racism and misogyny, antisemitism does not disappear just because you have correct politics. Antisemitism is an Othering force, a pull in language. Its manifestations need to be named and shamed, and its presence in our own hearts and ranks needs to be negotiated. And, sometimes, it must indeed result in forceful resistance of political enemies, of Others with whom political conversation must be rejected.⁵⁷

I close with a plea for doing that last only carefully, thoughtfully, cautiously. Where we sacrifice the possibility of persuasion, the resources of rhetoric as *"a symbolic means of inducing cooperation in beings that by nature respond to symbols,"* we sacrifice also the possibility of a larger community. Negotiating antisemitism, like the many other Othering swells that shape any given We, is an ongoing work. It is a work that can only be accomplished by a democratic people. If we are to become such a people, we will need both to reject Donald Trump's antisemitism and to rejectingly acknowledge our own. For this work, we need each other, and as many of our other Others as possible.

Notes

[1] This essay carefully sources arguable claims about who *said* what when, as well as about who *is* what and why (with an emphasis on informative over polemical media). I've cited almost exclusively from openly accessible sources so readers can comb through the data as desired. This is necessary for maintenance and reconstruction of an orientation toward truthfulness that is the mainstay of rhetorical theory, and that is critical for democracy. Too, though this essay was written in Spring 2017 and subsequent developments in American antisemitism have been dramatic (most notably, the events of August 2017 in Charlottesville, VA, including the vehicular murder of antifascist protester Heather Heyer by an aspiring neo-Nazi), I am sorry to say that developments have not outpaced the essay's basic argument. Nonetheless, in a longer, openly accessible piece, I do offer what I believe to be the fullest accounting of antisemitism's firing with Trumpism to date: see Ira J. Allen, "Donald Trump's Antisemitism — And Ours," *enculturation: a journal of rhetoric, writing, and culture*, forthcoming 2018.

[2] Framing such clashes as "devolving into violence" privileges a "free speech" reading of white supremacist organizing, and deprivileges an "incitement to violence" reading. For all Trump's invective against CNN, their reportage here was headlined by the obfuscating (in his supporters' favor) "Trump supporters, protesters clash in Berkeley"; no mention at all was made of antisemitism, and the signal instance of violence described was when "one man set afire a red 'USA' hat and held it overhead." See Ralph Ellis and Tony Marco, "Trump Supporters,

Protesters Clash in Berkeley," *CNN.com*, April 16, 2017, http://www.cnn.com/2017/04/15/us/berkeley-protests-trump/index.html. See also solidly liberal *Politico*'s sensational presentation of a bloodied Trumpist in its depiction of Berkeley as "a hotbed of violence," which "mainstream conservatives and liberals alike viewed… with trepidation, fearing their causes would be coopted by fringe elements." David Siders, "How Berkeley Became a Hotbed of Violence in the Trump Era," *Politico*, April 20, 2017, https://www.politico.com/story/2017/04/20/california-berkeley-coulter-protests-237424. In this rendering and many like it, violence is a by-product of extremists, while the event itself is normal political speech—"normal" in the peculiarly American sense of being divided neatly into two well-defined, opposing sides. Such a telling—which in the *Politico* story quotes sympathetically the Trumpists who marched and fought cheek-by-jowl with people waving Nazi flags—ignores entirely the togetherness of Trumpism and white supremacism at this and other such scenes.

3   "Based Stick Man—A Hero Arises," *Stormfront.com*, March 6, 2017, https://www.stormfront.org/forum/t1202578/.

4   Natasha Lennard, "The Violent Clashes in Berkeley Weren't 'Pro-Trump' Versus 'Anti-Trump'," *Esquire.com*, April 16, 2017, http://www.esquire.com/news-politics/news/a54564/the-violent-clashes-in-berkeley-werent-pro-trump-versus-anti-trump/.

5   Bay Area Proud Boys, Twitter post, April 15, 2017, https://twitter.com/ProudBoysCA/status/853426069831008258.

6   Richard Spencer, Twitter post, April 15, 2017, https://twitter.com/RichardBSpencer/status/853367105500188672.

7   Hunter Wallace, Twitter post, April 17, 2017, https://twitter.com/occdissent/status/854017853082697730.

8   Drew Harwell, Amy Brittain and Jonathan O'Connell, "Trump Family's Elaborate Lifestyle is a 'Logistical Nightmare'—At Taxpayer Expense," *Washington Post*, February 16, 2017, https://www.washingtonpost.com/business/economy/trump-familys-elaborate-lifestyle-a-logistical-nightmare--at-taxpayer-expense/2017/02/16/763cce8e-f2ce-11e6-a9b0-ecee7ce475fc_story.html.

9   Kenneth Burke, *A Rhetoric of Motives* (Berkeley, CA: University of California Press, 1950), 21.

10   Burke, *A Rhetoric of Motives*, 21.

11   Jessica Reaves, "White Supremacists Celebrate Trump's Victory," *Anti-Defamation League*, November 10, 2016, https://www.adl.org/blog/white-supremacists-celebrate-trumps-victory; Stephen Piggott, "White Nationalists and the So-Called 'Alt-Right' Celebrate Trump's Victory," *Southern Poverty Law Center*, November 9, 2016, https://www.splcenter.org/hatewatch/2016/11/09/white-nationalists-and-alt-right-celebrate-trump%E2%80%99s-victory.

12   For an informative, if polemical, take on key actors in America's newly

emboldened white supremacy movement, see online anarchist hub *It's Going Down*: "Meet the Neo-Nazis Who Organized the Klan-like Charlottesville, VA Rally," *ItsGoingDown.org*, May 15, 2017, https://itsgoingdown.org/meet-the-neo-nazis-responsible-for-holding-klan-like-rally-in-charlottesville-viginia/.

13 Sammy Nickals, "'Are Jews People' Was an Actual, Real Discussion Topic on CNN," *Esquire.com*, November 21, 2016, http://www.esquire.com/news-politics/news/a50906/are-jews-people-was-a-real/.

14 Justin Carissimo, "CNN Slammed for Running 'If Jews Are People' Headline," *The Independent*, November 22, 2016, http://www.independent.co.uk/arts-entertainment/tv/news/cnn-slammed-for-running-if-jews-are-people-headline-a7432146.html.

15 The ASDA'A Burson-Marsteller Arab Youth Survey for 2017 found that nearly two-thirds of Arabs between the ages of 18 and 24 felt concerned, scared, or angry about Trump's election—and that 70% believed him to be anti-Muslim (http://arabyouthsurvey.com/findings.html).

16 Aside from his long-time advocacy of birtherism, the racist insistence that President Obama could not really be American, there were many campaign rally comments like the cartoonishly stereotypical assertion that Black people, en masse, were "living in hell." See Jaweed Kaleem and Ann M. Simmons, "Trump Says African Americans Are Living in Hell. That Depends on What You Mean by Hell," *Los Angeles Times*, November 5, 2016, http://www.latimes.com/nation/la-na-global-black-america-snap-20161103-story.html.

17 On the way this taps into a distinctive rhetorical legacy, see Bruce Baum, "Donald Trump's 'Genius,' White 'Natural Aristocracy,' and Democratic Equality in America," *Theory & Event* 20.1 (2017): 10–22.

18 Jodi Kantor, "For Kushner, Israel Policy May Be Shaped by the Personal," *New York Times*, February 11, 2017, https://www.nytimes.com/2017/02/11/us/politics/jared-kushner-israel.html.

19 Sarah Begley, "Read Donald Trump's Speech to AIPAC," *Time*, March 21, 2016, http://time.com/4267058/donald-trump-aipac-speech-transcript/.

20 Tracy Wilkinson, "Israel Only Country to Escape Proposed Cuts to U.S. Foreign Aid," *Los Angeles Times*, March 16, 2017, http://www.latimes.com/politics/washington/la-na-essential-washington-updates-israel-only-country-to-escape-state-1489695965-htmlstory.html.

21 Anne Gearan and Ruth Eglash, "Trump Steps Back from US Commitment to Two-State Israeli-Palestinian Solution," *Washington Post*, February 15, 2017, https://www.washingtonpost.com/news/post-politics/wp/2017/02/15/trump-tells-netanyahu-to-hold-back-on-west-bank-settlements/.

22 Oren Liebermann, "The West Bank Settlement With Close Ties to Trump's Israel Envoy," *CNN.com*, March 9, 2017, http://www.cnn.com/2017/03/09/politics/west-bank-friedman-beit-el/.

23   David Gibson, "Trump Fails to Mention Jews in Holocaust Remembrance Statement," *USA Today*, January 27, 2017, https://www. usatoday.com/story/news/politics/2017/01/27/trump-fails-mention-jews-holocaust-remembrance-statement/97150252/. The Anne Frank Center for Mutual Respect described this omission as "a frightening echo of Holocaust deniers." See "President's Holocaust Remembrance Statement has a Dangerous Omission," *Anne Frank Center for Mutual Respect*, n.d., http://annefrank.com/presidents-holocaust-remembrance-statement-has-a-dangerous-omission/.

24   Stephen Collinson, "Trump Condemns Anti-Semitism But Can't Stop Questions about His Motives," *CNN.com*, February 21, 2017, http://www.cnn.com/2017/02/21/politics/donald-trump-anti-semitism-criticism/index.html.

25   Nathan Guttman, "Abe Foxman Says Wave of Anti-Semitic Hate Is No 'Crisis' — And Jews Should Lay Off Trump," *Forward.com*, March 2, 2017, http://forward.com/news/national/364765/abe-foxman-says-wave-of-anti-semitic-hate-is-no-crisis-and-jews-should-lay/.

26   "Is Donald Trump Another Jew-Puppet?" *Stormfront.com*, April 8, 2017, https://www.stormfront.org/forum/t1199800-24/.

27   "US Anti-Semitic Incidents Spike 86 Percent So Far in 2017 after Surging Last Year, ADL Finds," *Anti-Defamation League*, April 24, 2017, https://www.adl.org/news/press-releases/us-anti-semitic-incidents-spike-86-percent-so-far-in-2017.

28   "ADL Data Shows Anti-Semitic Incidents Continue Surge in 2017 Compared to 2016," *Anti-Defamation League*, November 2, 2017, https://www.adl.org/news/press-releases/adl-data-shows-anti-semitic-incidents-continue-surge-in-2017-compared-to-2016.

29   Frank S. Abderholden, "Officials: Lake County Bomb Threat May Be Part of National Anti-Semitic Campaign," *Chicago Tribune*, January 31, 2017, http://www.chicagotribune.com/suburbs/lake-county-news-sun/crime/ct-lns-anti-semitic-bomb-threats-st-0201-20170131-story.html. In a strange twist, it turned out most of these threats had been called in by a dual US/Israeli citizen, himself Jewish, calling from Israel. See Paul Goldman, Tom Winter, Pete Williams, and Erik Ortiz, "Israeli Police Arrest Suspect in Bomb Threats Made Against American Jewish Centers," *NBC News*, March 23, 2017, http://www.nbcnews.com/news/world/israeli-police-arrest-suspect-bomb-threats-made-against-american-jewish-n737581. A rhetorical perspective looks at the social effectivity of the calls (this has also been the position taken by the ADL). Alongside a massive spate of anti-Jewish vandalism, the cumulative effect of the bomb threats and reportage thereupon has been an uptick in the public presence of antisemitism.

30   "U.S. Anti-Semitic Incidents Spike 86 Percent So Far in 2017 After Surging Last Year, ADL Finds," *Anti-Defamation League*, April 24, 2017, https://www.adl.org/news/press-releases/us-anti-semitic-incidents-

spike-86-percent-so-far-in-2017.

31 "Anti-Semitic Incidents Spike in 2017, Especially after Charlottesville, Group Says," *CBS News*, November 2, 2017, https://www.cbsnews.com/news/adl-report-anti-semitic-incidents-spike-in-2017-especially-after-charlottesville/.

32 "ADL: White Supremacists Making Unprecedented Effort on U.S. College Campuses to Spread Their Message, Recruit," *Anti-Defamation League*, March 6, 2017, https://www.adl.org/news/press-releases/adl-white-supremacists-making-unprecedented-effort-on-us-college-campuses-to.

33 "Testimony of Jonathan A. Greenblatt, CEO and National Director, Anti-Defamation League, Before the Senate Judiciary Committee Hearings on Responses to Increase in Religious Hate Crimes," *Anti-Defamation League*, May 2, 2017, https://www.judiciary.senate.gov/imo/media/doc/05-02-17%20Greenblatt%20Testimony.pdf.

34 The ADL described this resistance as "mind-boggling." See "ADL: President Trump's Repeated Dodging of Serious Questions on Anti-Semitism Are 'Mind-Boggling'," *Anti-Defamation League*, February 16, 2017, https://www.adl.org/news/press-releases/adl-president-trumps-repeated-dodging-of-serious-questions-on-anti-semitism-are.

35 Eli Watkins, "Trump Tells Jewish Magazine's Reporter to 'Sit Down,' Blames Anti-Semitism on 'The Other Side'," *CNN.com*, February 16, 2017, http://www.cnn.com/2017/02/16/politics/donald-trump-news-conference-anti-semitism/index.html.

36 Watkins, "Trump Tells Jewish Magazine's Reporter to 'Sit Down.'"

37 Evan Osnos, "The Fearful and the Frustrated," *The New Yorker*, August 31, 2015, http://www.newyorker.com/magazine/2015/08/31/the-fearful-and-the-frustrated.

38 Andrew Anglin, "We Won," *Daily Stormer*, November 9, 2016, http://www.dailystormer.com/we-won/.

39 "Richard Spencer Punched in the Face," *Know Your Meme*, n.d., http://knowyourmeme.com/memes/richard-spencer-punched-in-the-face.

40 Glenn Kessler, "Donald Trump and David Duke: For the Record," *Washington Post*, March 1, 2016, https://www.washingtonpost.com/news/fact-checker/wp/2016/03/01/donald-trump-and-david-duke-for-the-record/.

41 Kessler, "Donald Trump and David Duke: For the Record."

42 Kessler, "Donald Trump and David Duke: For the Record."

43 As though determined to make matters worse, Spicer clarified that, although Hitler took "Jews into the Holocaust center," he at least "was not using the gas on his own people in the way that Assad is doing." See Jenna Johnson and Ashley Parker, "Spicer: Hitler 'Didn't Even Sink to Using Chemical Weapons,' Although He Sent Jews to 'the Holocaust Center,'" *Washington Post*, April 11, 2017, https://www.washington

post.com/news/post-politics/wp/2017/04/11/spicer-hitler-didnt-even-sink-to-using-chemical-weapons-although-he-sent-jews-to-the-holocaust-center/?tid=a_inl&utm_term=.f772d8e10a33.

44 Eileen Kane, "The Danger of Spicer's Casual Anti-Semitism," *The Hill*, April 27, 2017, http://thehill.com/blogs/pundits-blog/the-administration/330834-the-danger-of-spicers-casual-anti-semitism.

45 See, for instance, many of the episodes detailed in Leonard Dinnerstein's *Antisemitism in America* (New York: Oxford University Press, 1994). For a post-Charlottesville, popular take, see Rebecca Erbelding, "The Dark Political History of American Anti-Semitism," *The Hill*, August 21, 2017, http://thehill.com/blogs/pundits-blog/religion/347291-the-dark-political-history-of-american-anti-semitism.

46 Matthew Rozsa, "'What Universe Are These People Living In?' Anne Frank Center Blasts Sean Spicer for Complaints over Anti-Semitism Whitewash," *Salon*, February 22, 2017, http://www.salon.com/2017/02/22/what-universe-are-these-people-living-in-anne-frank-center-blasts-sean-spicer-for-complaints-over-anti-semitism-whitewash/.

47 For the former, in September 2016, see Amy Chozick, "Hillary Clinton Calls Many Trump Backers 'Deplorables,' and GOP Pounces," *New York Times*, September 10, 2016, https://www.nytimes.com/2016/09/11/us/politics/hillary-clinton-basket-of-deplorables.html; for the latter, see Hillary Clinton's September 2017 interview: David Remnick, "Hillary Clinton Looks Back in Anger," *The New Yorker*, September 25, 2017, https://www.newyorker.com/magazine/2017/09/25/hillary-clinton-looks-back-in-anger.

48 In support of the "deplorable" view, however, see Trevor Martin's latent semantic analysis for *FiveThirtyEight* of Trump supporters active on the subreddit /r/The_Donald, which finds dramatic overlaps for user participation in a range of other racist, sexist, and otherwise deplorable subreddits. Trevor Martin, "r/The_Donald," *FiveThirtyEight*, March 23, 2017, https://fivethirtyeight.com/features/dissecting-trumps-most-rabid-online-following/. Certainly, Clinton was entirely correct to call Trump himself deplorable, offensive, and dangerous.

49 *Vox*'s German Lopez offers a tightly factual summary of Donald Trump's long history of racism: German Lopez, "Donald Trump's Long History of Racism, From the 1970s to 2017," *Vox.com*, July 25, 2017, https://www.vox.com/2016/7/25/12270880/donald-trump-racism-history.

50 Chauncey DeVega, "10 Things Everyone Should Know About White Supremacy," *AlterNet*, April 23, 2014, http://www.alternet.org/civil-liberties/10-things-everyone-should-know-about-white-supremacy.

51 DeVega, "10 Things Everyone Should Know."

52 "ADL Poll: Anti-Semitic Attitudes in America Decline 3 Percent," *Anti-Defamation League*, October 28, 2013, https://www.adl.org/news/press-releases/adl-poll-anti-semitic-attitudes-in-america-decline-3-percent.

[53]   Burke, *A Rhetoric of Motives*, 25–26.

[54]   For anyone still skeptical on this score, see Ta-Nehisi Coates' instant classic, "The Case for Reparations," *The Atlantic*, June, 2014, https://www.theatlantic.com/magazine/archive/2014/06/the-case-for-reparations/361631/.

[55]   Different, that is, than the classic take offered by Jeffrey Tulis in the *The Rhetorical Presidency* (Princeton, NJ: Princeton University Press, 1987): that the American presidency is at base a position from which to *lead* public opinion. For more on this question, see also the essays in Ira Allen and Elizabeth Flynn (eds.), "Symposium: Barack Obama's Significance for Rhetoric and Composition," *College Composition and Communication* 67.3 (2016): 465–97.

[56]   This essay is offered in such a spirit, recalling particularly the skepticism of some conservative friends who doubt that there is anything meaningfully antisemitic about Trump.

[57]   To be clear, though, and as I have written elsewhere, democratic friendship cannot be understood to exclude violence absolutely. There are definitely times to punch Nazis. See Ira Allen, "On Nazi-Punching, Moral and Otherwise," *Medium*, April 19, 2017, https://medium.com/@beimpermissible/on-nazi-punching-moral-and-otherwise-4dc81b843d8b.

Ryan Skinnell

What Passes for Truth in the Trump Era: Telling It Like It Isn't

> *It turns out that the study of how to* uncover *deception is also by and large the study of how to* build up *fabrications.*
> *– Erving Goffman[1]*

Donald J. Trump is a notorious liar. Take, for instance, his entire presidential campaign. During the nearly 18-month election season, PolitiFact, a non-partisan, Pulitzer Prize-winning, fact-checking organization, rated him the most untruthful candidate out of a field of more than twenty candidates. Nearly 70% of his statements were rated "mostly false," "false," or "Pants-on-Fire! false."[2]

Trump's pattern of deception has continued uninterrupted into his presidency. Among his more egregious presidential mistruths, Trump openly lied about divesting himself of his business interests (he didn't), about his reasons for firing Federal Bureau of Investigation Director James Comey (he changed his story several times), and about the existence of 3–5 million fraudulent votes cast for Hillary Clinton during the election (a claim he continues to repeat periodically, despite a yawning lack of evidence).

In June 2017, just five months after his inauguration, the *New York Times* published a full-page "definitive list" of all Trump's lies since being sworn in.[3] In July, they felt compelled to publish an updated version. In October, the *Washington Post* published a similar catalogue.[4] Even though the *New York*

Times and *Washington Post* lists were limited to demonstrably false or misleading statements, both were impressively long. By the *Post*'s accounting, Trump had verifiably lied more than 1,300 times between his inauguration and mid-October, which averages out to more than five lies or misleading statements for every day he'd been in office to that point.

During Trump's administration, as during his campaign, professional fact-checkers are having a field day.[5] Likewise, members of the media—mostly on the left, but not exclusively—are hard at work trying to explain Trump's habitual dishonesty. Some of the more popular explanations include:

- He's a businessman[6]
- He's an entertainer[7]
- He's a narcissist[8]
- He's an idiot[9]
- He's just not interested in the truth[10]
- He uses lying as a weapon[11]
- He's committed to destroying the government[12]
- He's a fascist[13]
- He's a totalitarian[14]

Any of these may or may not explain Trump's relationship to lying and truth-telling. But frankly, it doesn't really matter. Proving Trump is a liar and/or explaining why he is a liar did not prevent him from being elected.

Trump lies because lying works, plain and simple. One reason, of course, is that a significant proportion of the American electorate didn't, and still doesn't, believe professional fact-checkers and the media. Or if they do, Trump's supporters believe him more, even when they know he is bending the truth. Bending the truth is one of his claims to success, as with his signature "truthful hyperbole."[15] In *The Art of the Deal*, he calls truthful hyperbole "an innocent form of exaggeration—and a very effective form of promotion" that plays to normal people's grandest fantasies.[16] In other words, Trump's truth-game as he explains it doesn't actually rely on people mistrusting the media (though it, of course, helps). For Trump's entire career, he's known that lying sells. In the last couple of years, business has been especially good. As a testament to this fact, many of his supporters and members of the media have routinely asserted that he should be taken "seriously, not literally." Another way of saying all of this is: a lot of people know he is lying, and they trust him anyway.

Given that reality, new questions arise: Why does Trump's lying work? Why do people still trust him even when they know he's lying? And why does every effort to demonstrate that he's a liar seem to fail, and, in some cases, even backfire? These questions are deceptively simple, but the answers are anything but self-evident.

Are Alternative Facts the Real Truth?

In late January 2017, shortly after Trump was sworn in as the 45th President of the United States, administration officials began aggressively claiming that Trump's inauguration was better attended than any previous inauguration. All the available evidence (photographs and video of the crowd, public transit statistics, estimates by knowledgeable experts, and so on) suggested he and his spokespeople were openly lying about the crowd size. It is anyone's guess why he was so insistent about winning the crowd size competition. In any case, Trump and his press secretary and a significant proportion of his media representatives repeated the lie over and over and over again.

One of Trump's top campaign and administration advisors, Kellyanne Conway, was finally confronted about the lie on *Meet the Press* two days after the inauguration. Rather than admit it was a lie and attempt to walk it back, however, Conway doubled down. She even whipped up a handy catchphrase to explain her energetic defense of the claim: the administration supposedly had access to "alternative facts."[17]

Conway's "alternative facts" is just one example among many of the Trump team's perverse reversal of truth and lies, but it helpfully illustrates several points. Among them, Trump and his surrogates simply do not accept that they should feel ashamed for lying, even when they're caught and confronted.

In this, they are radically different from the vast majority of American politicians.

This may seem like an extreme claim. After all, every politician lies. For instance, although Trump was the lying-est liar in the 2016 campaign, none of the candidates were 100% honest. Even the least deceitful candidates in the presidential campaign, regardless of party, lied about 25% of the time.[18] As voters, Americans have long accepted that politicians lie as part of the democratic bargain. Presumably, this is because candidates feel like they have to pander to voters, and maybe even mislead voters in the process, in order to get elected. But even among politicians, Trump's lying is unusual.[19]

Most obviously, he's shameless. Although lying is a common ingredient in American politics, and probably all politics since the dawn of time, most politicians at least pay lip service to the importance of telling the truth. And, as a result, most politicians at least pretend to be ashamed when they get caught in a lie. Not so with Trump and his associates. The fight over the size of his inauguration crowd is Exhibit A, but there are many more analogous exhibits than there are letters in the alphabet.

But establishing that Trump is a serial liar only gets us so far. America's politics and our government institutions presume truth-telling on the part of public servants. By and large, American laws and customs are designed to assume that people are acting in good faith until there is definitive proof to the contrary. Americans likewise assume that candidates and officials will accept the value of truth and will act accordingly. In this case, "accordingly" means accepting shame if they are caught lying, changing their behaviors (at least outwardly), and maybe even leaving office, as in the cases of disgraced politicians such as Richard Nixon, Newt Gingrich, and Anthony Weiner. As it turns out, the formal processes for punishing lying are actually relatively difficult to initiate because everyone seems to assume they'll only be necessary in extreme cases.

None of this is to say Americans aren't cynical about politicians' relationship to truth — quite the contrary — only that truth is the baseline expectation, and violations are generally seen as just that. In other words, even though American voters accept that politicians often lie, they also operate on a fundamental expectation of truth-telling and good faith. The expectation of truth-telling and good faith is what makes catching a politician in a lie scandalous, and ironically is also what makes actively penalizing liars something of a challenge.

In addition, the majority of American voters, members of the media, and other politicians simply do not have good tools for understanding Trump's lying. As I mentioned above, fact-checkers and members of the media have been calling him a liar — with several decades worth of unimpeachable evidence — at least since he announced his candidacy in June of 2015. All to little effect. Calling Donald J. Trump a liar and proving he is a liar do not seem to result in any direct consequences or noticeable changes in his behavior. Trump lies, his advisors and spokespeople reiterate the lie, and when confronted with contrary evidence they defend the lie. If anything, as his administration progresses and as he keeps getting away with lying, his lies become more audacious.

For that matter, even when his supporters accept that he is a liar, they do not necessarily stop supporting him. Take, for example, Trump supporter and former Congressman Joe Walsh's August 2017 tweet:

Fig. 1: Joe Walsh tweet.[20]

Apparently for Walsh, Trump's lying makes him decent and trustworthy because he's honest about lying—if nothing else, you can trust him to lie. It is certainly the case that some people are deceived by his lying.[21] But it is also the case that many of his supporters, like Walsh, acknowledge he is lying and, on the basis of this acknowledgement, they believe him to be even more trustworthy. It is not that Trump's supporters can't discern lies—rather, it seems to be that they are largely unconvinced that his lying is a problem. On its face, it is a baffling, and frankly alarming, sort of logic. But baffling and alarming does not mean uncommon or inconsequential.

For those of us who are dismayed by Trump's chronic lying, the easiest source of comfort is to believe his supporters are either (a) stupid or (b) evil. Those are the two most obvious threads in the unrelenting glut of "get to know Trump supporters" op-eds and profiles produced following his election. The implication is that Trump only dishes out falsehoods that flatter his supporters and attack his opponents. The villains don't care because they're profiting and the rubes eat it up.[22]

Comforting though this belief may be, however, it's pretty hard to maintain if we accept that his supporters know he's lying, and as the Walsh example shows, there is good reason to believe they do. In other words, the majority of Trump's supporters are not stupid. Frankly, they're mostly not evil, either.

What We Talk About When We Talk About "Truth"

So where does this leave us? The United States of America has a president who lies as a matter of course, a gang of deputies who eagerly reinforce his lies, a system that is not well designed to force him to tell the truth, and, most impressively, an audience of supporters who know he's lying but trust him anyway. Night is day, up is down, black is white.

If we want to understand "truth" in these circumstances, it turns out the ancient study of rhetoric has some useful tools.

Rhetoric often gets a bad rap as an art of deception—Plato, for example, accused rhetoricians of being in the business of making the weaker argument appear the stronger. Some 2,000+ years later, accusing a person of using rhetoric retains the allegation of trickery and dishonesty. Modern day rhetoric scholars take issue with that characterization of rhetoric—we profess to study persuasive language in all its forms. But deception is undoubtedly one of language's many persuasive forms. As such, rhetoricians have learned a thing or two about deceptive language over the years, and we've developed some useful concepts for understanding how it works.

To begin with, rhetoric teaches us that we can think about truth—or in Trump's case, lying—in at least two registers. The first is in terms of content; the second is what we might call a statement's social function. Judged on content alone, Trump is one of the least truthful major politicians in modern American history. There is no indication that he or his followers are troubled by this status. Indeed, even before he was inaugurated, Kellyanne Conway scolded news outlets like CNN for trying to restrict him to truthful content. On January 9, 2017, in a defense of Trump's tweet claiming that he never mocked a disabled reporter (of which there is video evidence), Conway told CNN's Chris Cuomo, "You always want to go by what's come out of his mouth rather than look at what's in his heart."[23] Truthful content is clearly not the main objective here.

The second register is how a statement acts as a kind of social truth, independent of the specific content. In the case of Conway's declaration, the social function of Trump's tweeted truth is roughly analogous to "what's in his heart"—what he *means* instead of what he actually *says*. Journalists and political opponents usually attempt to evaluate Trump's content, which is how political truths are usually evaluated. But if we're supposed to go by "what's in [Trump's] heart" instead of "what's come out of his mouth," understanding this second register of truth can help us make better sense of Donald Trump's habitual lying.

Trump's commitment to "truthful hyperbole," in particular, gives us a clue to how this second register of truth works. Hyperbole is the intentional use of wildly exaggerated statements. Rather than say "I'm very hungry," for instance, a person might say, "I'm so hungry I could eat a horse." One key to hyperbole is that hyperbolic statements are not supposed to be taken literally—the exaggeration is so over-the-top that it would be ridiculous to take the claim at face value. We generally do not believe that our dinner companion will consume an entire horse.

In the case of hyperbole, Trump is actually not incorrect to call it "truthful." For rhetoric scholars, hyperbolic over-exaggeration brings out a kind of truth by emphasizing a claim's emotional dimensions. "I'm very hungry" may be technically factual, but it does not explain the emotional depth of the truth. "I could eat a horse" better indicates how the speaker experiences the feeling of hunger—that is, intensely. Hyperbole brings an underlying truth to the surface that the factual truth can't quite describe.

Trump is, of course, a master of hyperbole. His campaign slogan, for instance, promises to "Make American Great Again!" On standards of content, it's patently ridiculous. But as hyperbole, it's not terribly hard to tease out the meaning. His supporters feel like *something* is really wrong, and Trump both sees it and claims he can fix it. The same kind of "truth" is apparent in his assertions about things being "tremendous," "yuge," and "the biggest ever." On a recent visit to Asia, Trump claimed that his reception was unprecedented: "It was red carpet like nobody, I think, has probably ever seen."[24] Here again, the content doesn't hold up to scrutiny, but Trump's point is not necessarily to prove *the* truth so much as to prove *a* truth—he was treated like royalty by the host countries because he is so terribly important. His claim really does tell us so much more than, "I received a very nice welcome." The hyperbolic overstatement is much better suited to communicating the feeling—both his and what he thinks ours should be—of his treatment than any straightforward reportage of the facts ever could.

Frank or Fearless Speech

Useful as hyperbole is for understanding Trump's particular brand of truth-telling, it does not tell us the whole truth—or even the most important truth—about his lying because it is, at heart, a kind of truth-telling. In other words, hyperbole explains his exaggeration of the truth, but not what is so persuasive about his outright, obvious lies. For this, a more useful rhetorical concept is *parrhēsia* (pronounced: par-rhay-see'-ah).

Parrhēsia is an Ancient Greek term that translates roughly as "the freedom to speak." It is not exactly the equivalent of Americans' Constitutional freedom of speech, however. Parrhēsia entails somewhat different connotations than the 1st Amendment. In fact, parrhēsia ends up being a slightly complicated concept, but for the time being a quick and dirty definition is a good place to start. Parrhēsia is "frank or fearless speech," with the implication of someone speaking truth to power even in the face of potentially serious consequences.

According to historian of rhetoric Arthur Walzer, parrhēsia has two primary forms. One is that of "a counselor offering frank criticism of a prince in a monarchical context."[25] In this first form of parrhēsia, it is common to think of a king's royal advisor as an example—someone who is willing, even potentially at the cost of his or her life, to tell the emperor flatly that the supreme ruler is not wearing any clothes. In this context, parrhēsia has a sort of underdog quality that is appealing to a lot of Americans—the notion that someone with little or no power will speak the candid truth to an oppressive, dominating leader in service to the greater good is a romantic one.

But the second form of parrhēsia is actually more appropriate in 21st-century America. Walzer's second form of parrhēsia is of "an orator criticizing the *demos* in a democratic political context." This is where it gets a little complicated. In this second form, the person engaged in parrhēsia—the parrhēsiastes—risks his or her reputation to confront not the ruler, but the *demos*—that is, the common people. In a democracy, rulers are supposed to be subject to the will of the citizens they represent. Parrhēsiatic speech is, therefore, directed at citizens because they hold power by way of their vote.

There are fewer obvious, visible examples of this second form of parrhēsia, in part because the first form is so idealized and in part because it can be hard to distinguish when a parrhēsiastes is speaking hard truths to society. Nevertheless, some enlightening examples do exist.

Take Muhammad Ali. In 1966, the American War in Vietnam had its highest approval ratings in the United States—more than half of Americans approved of the war. Ali was eligible to be drafted to fight in Vietnam, but he openly and publicly refused to report for duty, famously asking, "Why should they ask me to put on a uniform and go ten thousand miles from home and drop bombs and bullets on brown people in Vietnam while so-called Negro people in Louisville are treated like dogs and denied simple human rights?"

Ali spent four years in court battles over his refusal to join the US military, during which time he also lost his boxing license, millions of dollars of income, and much of his public favor. Despite the real personal and professional consequences, however, Ali waged an open, public, anti-war campaign from 1966-1971, when the Supreme Court finally overturned his conviction. Ali did famously speak truth to power—to Lyndon Johnson and military leaders, for example—but his most consequential, and most frank, parrhēsiatic activity was directed more broadly at the *demos*—that is, at Americans who believed that the war in Vietnam was just and necessary. Ali openly accused Americans who supported the war of harboring racist, colonialist, and discriminatory beliefs, not just against the Vietnamese, but also against African-Americans. Over time Ali was credited with turning sentiment against the war, but he suffered significantly as a result. Although he was not a politician that lost votes, Ali nevertheless offers us a good example of parrhēsia in that he accepted the responsibility and consequences of his frank and fearless speech.

Without losing sight of the differences between our two forms of parrhēsia, an important point to take from Walzer's definition is that in either form parrhēsia requires (1) frank speech, (2) risk or danger for the speaker, (3) an unwavering duty to society, and (4) the expression of fundamental truths. Taken together, these characteristics of parrhēsia signal the speaker's virtue.

Trump, the Parrhēsiastes

It is tempting at this point to ask if Donald Trump is a faithful parrhēsiastes. He is nothing if not frank and fearless. He's a self-styled fearless speaker—unafraid to tell it like it is, unbeholden to the political elites. This is not only one of his signature assertions about himself, but it is also one of the characteristics that his many supporters claim to love about him. He is not overly rehearsed and he is definitely not "politically correct." During his campaign, he often claimed he was willing to risk his fortune, his reputation, and his business and media empire to make America great again.

At the same time, there are ways in which our definition of parrhēsia raises as many questions as it answers. Trump speaks frankly, but does he really accept any risk? Potentially, but probably not the kind of risk that, say, a court jester faces when confronting an unstable and spiteful prince. Trump zealously claims a duty to society, but is he sincerely expressing fundamental truths? It is an interesting thought experiment, but probably not a very satisfying one in the long run.

In fact, following the impulse to prove Trump is or isn't a faithful parrhēsiastes would be a mistake. Proving that Trump does or does not live up to the true definition of parrhēsia leads us back into the trap of believing that we can somehow delegitimize him by showing that he's not what he seems to be. But it didn't work during the campaign and it won't work now. A more useful question we might ask is: "What does the concept of parrhēsia offer us to help us better understand the force of his appeals?"

The answer, perhaps surprisingly, is in the anticipated outcome of parrhēsia—the demonstration of virtue. In his recent study of Ancient Greek demagoguery, Gottfried Mader makes an important distinction between populists and parrhēsiasi. Whereas populists supposedly pander to their audiences, parrhēsiasi confront their audiences bluntly as a demonstration of independence.[26] In other words, parrhēsiasi are not afraid to tell their audiences the harsh truth. At first blush, this description may not seem applicable to Trump, who is so notably quick to attack his opponents. For instance, he is fond of conjuring evil PC liberal elites as targets he can attack— Crooked Hillary, Pocahontas (Elizabeth Warren), Crazy Bernie, and Fake Tears Chuck Schumer, for example. Or Rosie O'Donnell. Or Nancy Pelosi. Or Barack Obama.

But Trump also has a habit of attacking his supposed allies, including the people in his crowds. On the stump, he regularly asserted, "America doesn't win anymore,"[27] "Our country is going to hell,"[28] and "America is weak and ineffective."[29] He's taken high-profile swipes at veterans (including soldiers killed in action) and their families, at FOX News, at American intelligence agencies, and at Republican Party leadership. In angry tweets, Trump has derisively called Senate Majority Leader and supposed ally, Republican Mitch McConnell, "Mr. Repeal & Replace" and "The Work Shirker," as part of accusations that McConnell is incompetent and ineffectual. And in September 2017, Trump even aligned with Democrats against Republicans to pass a multi-billion dollar fiscal plan.[30] He's openly threatened riots on more than one occasion. He's talked about his supporters as illiterate, uneducated, and blindly loyal. He's insulted American allies on a frighteningly regular basis, and he semi-regularly threatens to cut off support for any and all Republicans who don't fight hard enough to protect him or advocate for his wishes.

At this point, it is totally unsurprising when he insults his opponents, but in his speeches and rallies he also routinely insults members of his own audience by implying that they're weak, ineffective losers. In other words, while the assumption is that Trump traffics only in flattery, a good deal of what he says actually implicates and even insults his supporters.

The point here is that we cannot simply chalk his supporters' blind loyalty to him up to his mutual loyalty to them. He's quixotic at the best of times. Likewise, we cannot chalk his lying up to his efforts to get one over on his opponents as a demonstration of his loyalty to his supporters. He insults everybody. He lies to everybody. He's shameless about both. His lies are not simply to placate his base. Like his insults, Trump's lies are clearly in service to his own (shifting) goals, irrespective of anyone else's and irrespective of anything he may previously have claimed or may claim in the future. All the more reason to wonder why some people remain faithful to him even when they know he ultimately can't be trusted to have their best interests at heart.

The answer is frankness.

Where parrhēsia is concerned, frankness is the speaker's chief virtue. "The [parrhēsiatic] speaker is supposed to give a complete and exact account of what he has in mind so the audience is able to comprehend exactly what the speaker thinks... And he does this by avoiding any kind of rhetorical form, which would veil what he thinks. Instead, the parrhēsiastes uses the most direct words and forms of expression he can find... and acts on other people's minds by showing them as directly as possible what he actually believes."[31]

Here we might refer back to Kellyanne Conway's instruction to "look at what's in his heart." Trump may be an unrepentant liar but, according to Conway, Walsh, and many of his supporters, he is only a liar because he is so transparently truthful. Political writer Eve Peyser, a critic of Trump, seems to agree: "Trump is a liar, but since he doesn't have a filter, he manages to lie authentically."[32] Likewise, Virginia Heffernan at *Politico* goes so far as to claim that Trump can't lie, even when he should. "No matter the stakes, he doesn't have even a White

House junior aide's gift for circumspection, spin or truth-shading. Lately, in fact, Trump can't shut up even when almost *everything* is at stake."[33]

Trump is a liar. But he is a ridiculously bad liar because he is so emotionally transparent. And his emotional transparency causes him to speak frankly and fearlessly, even to his allies, even to his supporters, even when it could potentially harm him. We might wonder why it has not (yet) doomed him, as it has many other politicians.

Here we can add one more wrinkle to our working definition of parrhēsia. We have already set out two forms—the frank and fearless speech of (1) an advisor to a powerful ruler, or (2) an orator criticizing the *demos*. In both of these cases, the parrhēsiastes finds him or herself pulled into a position where they feel compelled to speak the truth. In the 1980s, however, French philosopher Michel Foucault wrote a critical study of parrhēsia that introduces a new point of consideration. According to Foucault, a person—a prince for instance—might actually seek out a parrhēsiates. The goal was to get someone who would offer an honest account of the prince's flaws so that the prince can work to become more virtuous. In other words, the modern way of imagining parrhēsia is as a thing an actor feels compelled to perform in the face of a powerful audience. So we might think again of Trump telling the painful truth to his listeners.

But in this other, ancient model, the ruler or the audience seeks out a parrhēsiastes for useful—if nevertheless potentially painful—feedback. As Foucault put it, "parrhēsia is the courage of truth in the person who speaks and who, regardless of everything, takes the risk of telling the whole truth that he thinks. But it is also the interlocutor's courage in agreeing to accept the hurtful truth he hears."[34] The speaker tells the hard truth, but the listener has to be willing to hear it. In the parrhēsiatic game, when both speaker and audience accept the terms of engagement where one speaks frankly and the other accepts the hurtful truth, insults can strengthen the relationship because both the speaker and audience accept the risks and responsibilities of frankness. It is at this point that we can begin to really understand Donald Trump's lying.

When we consider this last sense of parrhēsia, we can see how Trump actually bolsters his appeal by denigrating his audiences. He is virtuous in his fearlessness and frankness, even toward his own supporters, which buys him the kind of ironic goodwill he needs to say virtually whatever he wants to or about virtually anyone else. He's bestowing on them a kind of tough love—one his audiences seem to appreciate enough to disregard any factual lies he tells.

Now What?

At minimum, the concept of parrhēsia invites us to think a little differently about how a speaker relates to an audience and vice versa. It's not just a matter of telling people what they want to hear. It might also include telling supporters that they're not actually all that great. It may actually mean telling your base that they've been uneducated, weak, unprincipled suckers. Making America great again is not just about wiping the floor with the people on the other team—it includes that, but in this case it is also about pointing to your own team's obvious deficiencies and demonstrating you're not afraid to fix them. That you're the only one who really can fix them, in fact. The evidence is in your willingness to point out the flaws—fearlessly and frankly—in the first place.

Of course, identifying parrhēsia does not stop it. Nor does it counteract Trump's lying. But identifying parrhēsia in Donald J. Trump's appeals does give us some options for moving forward. For one, there is ample evidence that Trump's supporters are not just suckers who are falling for a scam. Some may be uninformed, of course, but most seem to know that Trump is an inveterate liar, at least on the level of content. They are quite often not taken in by his lies, and they have supported him despite his penchant for dishonesty. What this means is that education campaigns to inform Trump supporters are more often than not time wasted. As well, "getting to know" Trump supporters misses the point, and as a number of other contributors here make plain, simply cutting Trumpists off isn't a viable answer, either.

For some Trump opponents, this realization may be distressing, but it shouldn't be. In fact, identifying parrhēsia helps us recognize ways Trump and his auditors genuinely believe themselves to be engaged in a truth-telling relationship. In other words, even though most Trumpists are not suckers, most are also not cynical opportunists, either. Rather, they definitely value "truth," at least of a certain sort. And that certain sort of truth is not simple flattery or indulgence. It is not (experienced as) nuanced or carefully couched or indirect or veiled. Instead, it is a hard sort of fundamental truth—what we might in a different context compare to breaking someone down to build them up or even "tough love"—that acknowledges risk or danger for the speaker and an unwavering duty to society. From a certain perspective, Trump shamed his supporters. But even if that is so, he shamed them in ways that they experienced as frank and fearless and devoted, not insulting and demoralizing. That's a lesson we can and should learn from Trump the Parrhēsiastes.

I'll stop here by noting that this parrhēsiatic relationship—one that includes insult, directness, even open humiliation of one's closest human contacts—is hardly limited to Trump. We see it in all sorts of politics, entertainment, and even education. I would even suggest, given social media's centrality to the current moment, it is one of the signature forms of human interaction in 21st-century American culture. Recognizing Donald J. Trump's intuitive skill for delivering frank speech, then, suggests that truth—of the hard, but also caring kind—needs to be reinvigorated as an important part of American politics. Filter bubbles have their limits, but so does compassion. There is an important space for frankness and candor in American politics if it commits to the virtues of parrhēsia: risk or danger for the speaker, an unwavering duty to society, and the expression of fundamental truths. Perhaps this realization can help us recognize different ways to engage in

American democracy—and American political discussions—
moving forward.

Notes

[1]   Erving Goffman, *Frame Analysis* (New York: Basic Books, 1974), 14.
[2]   "Donald Trump's File," *Politifact*, n.d., http://www.politifact.com/
      personalities/donald-trump/.
[3]   David Leonhardt and Stuart A. Thompson, "President Trump's Lies,
      the Definitive List," *New York Times*, June 23, 2017, https://www.ny
      times.com/interactive/2017/06/23/opinion/trumps-lies.html.
[4]   Michelle Hee Lee, Glenn Kessler, and Meg Kelly, "President Trump Has
      Made 1,318 False or Misleading Claims over 263 Days," *Washington
      Post*, October 10, 2017, https://www.washingtonpost.com/news/fact-
      checker/wp/2017/10/10/president-trump-has-made-1318-false-or-
      misleading-claims-over-263-days/?utm_term=.208a5d343f71.
[5]   For some of the more professional examples, see "Donald Trump's
      File," *Politifact*, n.d., http://www.politifact.com/personalities/donald-
      trump/; "Donald Trump," *FactCheck.org*, n.d., http://www.factcheck.
      org/person/donald-trump/; Glenn Kessler, "Fact Checker: The Truth
      Behind the Rhetoric," *Washington Post*, n.d., https://www.washington
      post.com/news/fact-checker/wp/category/donald-trump.
[6]   David Barstow, "Up Is Down: Trump's Unreality Show Echoes His
      Business Past," *New York Times*, January 28, 2017, https://www.ny
      times.com/2017/01/28/us/politics/donald-trump-truth.html.
[7]   Kareem Abdul-Jabbar, "Which Is Worse? That Donald Trump Lies So
      Much, or That He's So Bad at Lying?" *The Hollywood Reporter*, June 1,
      2016, http://www.hollywoodreporter.com/news/is-worse-donald-
      trump-lies-898514.
[8]   Dana Milbank, "Of Course Trump Called Comey a Liar: That's Always
      Been His Strategy," *Washington Post*, June 12, 2017, https://www.
      washingtonpost.com/opinions/of-course-trump-called-comey-a-liar-
      thats-his-strategy/2017/06/12/6ff4b4a8-4fa6-11e7-91eb-9611861a988f
      _story.html?utm_term=.c38a05d5a02b.
[9]   Robyn Urback, "Take It from the Republican Faithful—Trump's Not a
      Liar, Just an Idiot," *CBC News*, June 8, 2017, http://www.cbc.ca/news/
      opinion/trump-comey-testimony-1.4152589.
[10] Matthew Yglesias, "The Bullshitter-in-Chief," *Vox*, May 30, 2017,
      https://www.vox.com/policy-and-politics/2017/5/30/15631710/
      trump-bullshit.
[11] Charles M. Blow, "Trump Isn't Hitler. But the Lying?" *New York Times*,
      October 19, 2017, https://www.nytimes.com/2017/10/19/opinion/
      trump-isnt-hitler-but-the-lying.html.
[12] Jack Goldsmith, "Will Donald Trump Destroy the Presidency?" *The
      Atlantic*, October, 2017, https://www.theatlantic.com/magazine/
      archive/2017/10/will-donald-trump-destroy-the-presidency/537921/.

13 Renowned Holocaust historian, Timothy Snyder, put it this way
    recently: "As I see it, there are certainly elements of his approach which
    are fascistic. The straight-on confrontation with the truth is at the center
    of the fascist worldview. The attempt to undo the Enlightenment as a
    way to undo institutions, that is fascism." Chauncey DeVega,
    "Historian Timothy Snyder: 'It's Pretty Much Inevitable' That Trump
    Will Try to Stage a Coup...," *Salon*, May 1, 2017, https://www.salon.
    com/2017/05/01/historian-timothy-snyder-its-pretty-much-inevitable-
    that-trump-will-try-to-stage-a-coup-and-overthrow-democracy/.

14 Austin Sarat, "Trump's Totalitarian Impulse," *US News*, May 17, 2017,
    https://www.usnews.com/opinion/thomas-jefferson-street/articles/
    2017-05-16/donald-trumps-totalitarian-threat-to-fbi-director-james-
    comey.

15 Jane Mayer, "Donald Trump's Ghostwriter Tells All," *The New Yorker*,
    July 25, 2016, http://www.newyorker.com/magazine/2016/07/25/
    donald-trumps-ghostwriter-tells-all.

16 Donald J. Trump, *The Art of the Deal* (New York: Random House, 2009),
    58. Trump is not the first person to note the value of exaggeration.
    Writing more than two millennia ago, Aristotle notes, hyperboles
    "show vehemence of character; and this is why angry people use them
    more than other people." Aristotle, *On Rhetoric: A Theory of Civic Dis-
    course*, trans. George A. Kennedy (Oxford: Oxford University Press,
    2007), 130.

17 "Conway: Press Secretary Gave 'Alternative Facts'," *Meet the Press*, NBC
    News, January 22, 2017, https://www.nbcnews.com/meet-the-press/
    video/conway-press-secretary-gave-alternative-facts-860142147643.

18 In August 2016, blogger Robert Mann created a data visualization of
    PolitiFact's truth ratings of the major presidential candidates to that
    point. The chart Mann created was shared extensively on social media
    and subjected to its own fact checks. Other journalists, bloggers, and
    consultants have conducted similar studies to much the same conclu-
    sions, give or take a few percentage points. Robert Mann, "Who Lies
    More: A Comparison," *Mann Metrics*, August 5, 2016, http://mann
    metrics.com/who-lies-more/.

19 Maria Konnikova, "Trump's Lies Vs. Your Brain," *Politico*, January/
    February 2017, https://www.politico.com/magazine/story/2017/01/
    donald-trump-lies-liar-effect-brain-214658.

20 Joe Walsh, Twitter post, August 2, 2017, https://twitter.com/walsh
    freedom/status/892752848114651137?lang=en.

21 George Lakoff and Elisabeth Wehling, *Your Brain's Politics: How the
    Science of Mind Explains the Political Divide* (Exeter: Societas, 2016).

22 Genocide scholar James Waller describes the social psychology of in-
    group/out-group relations. Essentially, in its extreme form, we believe
    people who are like us are good and people who aren't are bad. And we
    believe people who are in our in-groups are more like us than they

actually are and people who are in out-groups are more similar to each other (and less similar to us) than they actually are. Intense in-group/out-group behaviors have thrived in America in the past 30 years, and they have been heightened even further in the Trump era. James Waller, *Confronting Evil: Engaging Our Responsibility to Prevent Genocide* (Oxford: Oxford University Press, 2016).

23 Eric Bradner, "Conway on Streep's Criticism: 'Is It Always Appropriate to Talk Politics?'" *CNN.com*, January 9, 2017, http://www.cnn.com/2017/01/09/politics/kellyanne-conway-trump-meryl-streep/index.html.

24 Allan Smith, "Trump Lauds the Special Treatment He Got in Asia: 'It Was Red Carpet Like Nobody, I Think, Has Probably Ever Seen'," *Business Insider*, November 13, 2017, http://www.businessinsider.com/trump-asia-red-carpet-china-vietnam-2017-11.

25 Arthur E. Walzer, "Parrēsia, Foucault, and the Classical Rhetorical Tradition," *Rhetoric Society Quarterly* 43:1 (2013), 1.

26 Gottfried Mader, "Demagogic Style and Historical Method: Locating Cleon's Mytilenean Rhetoric (Thucydides 3.37–40)," *Rhetorica* 35.1 (2017), 8.

27 Tim Hains, "Trump on Perpetual War: 'We Don't Win Anymore, We Just Fight, Like Vomiting, Fight, Fight, Fight'," *RealClearPolitics*, February 9, 2016, https://www.realclearpolitics.com/video/2016/02/09/trump_we_dont_win_wars_anymore_we_just_fight_like_vomiting_fight_fight_fight.html.

28 "RUSH Transcript: Donald Trump//CNN Republican Presidential Town Hall Columbia, SC," *CNN Press Room*, February 18, 2016, http://cnnpressroom.blogs.cnn.com/2016/02/18/rush-transcript-donald-trump-cnn-republican-presidential-town-hall-columbia-sc/.

29 Jeremy Diamond, "Donald Trump on Torture: 'We Have to Beat the Savages' Politics," *CNN.com*, March 6, 2016, http://www.cnn.com/2016/03/06/politics/donald-trump-torture/index.html.

30 Mike DeBonis, Kelsey Snell, Philip Rucker, and Elise Viebeck, "Trump Sides with Democrats on Fiscal Issues, Throwing Republican Plans into Chaos," *Washington Post*, September 6, 2017, https://www.washingtonpost.com/powerpost/house-prepares-for-harvey-relief-vote/2017/09/06/62919058-92fc-11e7-89fa-bb822a46da5b_story.html?utm_term=.4b7a31f8f71a.

31 Michel Foucault, *Fearless Speech* (Cambridge: MIT Press, 2001), 12.

32 Eve Peyser, "The Strange Appeal of Trump's 'Honest' Lies," *Vice*, August 3, 2017, https://www.vice.com/en_us/article/bjzg98/the-strange-appeal-of-trumps-honest-lies.

33 Virginia Heffernan, "Trump Is America's Most Honest President," *Politico*, May 23, 2017, http://www.politico.com/magazine/story/2017/05/23/trump-is-americas-most-honest-president-215180.

34 Michel Foucault, *The Courage of Truth* (New York: Picador, 2011), 13.

Patricia Roberts-Miller

Charisma Isn't Leadership, and Other Lessons We Can Learn from Trump the Businessman

In the summer of 2017, various right-wing media engaged in an instance of heavy-rotation moral panic. The New York Shakespeare in the Park had performed *Julius Caesar*, and the Caesar character looked like Donald Trump. The right-wing media managed to get a lot of people with strong opinions and not a lot of information to be outraged on the grounds that Caesar/Trump is killed.[1] The outragees weren't offended by the comparison to Shakespeare's representation of Caesar, since they clearly didn't know what that representation was (Shakespeare's Caesar is neither a villain nor tyrant), but were instead angered by some vague sense that 1) the character who looks like Trump dies, and 2) librul eggheads.

I will argue that the Shakespeare in the Park episode, in a nutshell, is how "reasoning" works in the highly authoritarian identity politics of charismatic leadership. Charismatic leadership, which I define in more detail below, is a relationship that depends on what scholars in rhetoric call "identification," in which a person or group of people (Trump supporters, in this case) feel themselves to be "substantially one" with the leader.[2]

Of course, neither authoritarianism nor charismatic leadership is specific to right-wing media — Mao Tse Tung, Joseph Stalin, and Che Guevara are left-wing authoritarian leaders with a charismatic leadership relationship to their followers—but current assumptions in American business and popular culture make it somewhat more likely for charismatic leadership to be functional on the right than left.

We are at a nasty moment for democracy, and it is partially the consequence of a pernicious equation—charismatic leadership is good for business + government should be run more like businesses = therefore, charismatic leadership must be good for government.

Briefly, my argument is that charismatic leadership is not necessarily good for business, and its tendency toward authoritarianism makes it actively dangerous as a basis for democratic policymaking. But all of that tends to get lost because 1) people conflate "a leader with charisma" and "charismatic leadership," 2) people ignore the dark side of a relationship that silences dissent, precludes criticism, and is grounded in subverting critical thinking to pure identification, and 3) people throw around the term "authoritarianism" to mean "a leader forcing policies on me I don't like."

Leaders with Charisma
versus Charismatic Leadership

A basic question for a reasonably large group of people with a common purpose (a village, state, company, church, business) is how to get people to comply with the rules. That question is sometimes phrased as a question of "authority" (what authority do individuals give the community's rules) but it can also be phrased as a question of "legitimacy" (what rules do individuals consider legitimate and why).

Imagine that there is a rule in a company that people have to turn in TPS reports on a weekly basis, and those reports need to be done a particular way. An individual, let's call him Chester, might comply with that practice for any one of various reasons:

1) Blind obedience (it never occurs to him to do anything other than what he has been told to do);

2) Habit or apathy (he has gotten accustomed to doing them, and doesn't think about it much);
3) Tradition or ritual (it is a mark of group loyalty to do the reports, or doing them is seen as a tribal ritual);
4) Fear of punishment (he does it because he doesn't want to get yelled at, or there is a large fine for failing to do the reports);
5) Strategic acquiescence (he doesn't like doing the reports, but he believes it will make his boss like him, it might help him get a raise, or he doesn't feel like going to the trouble of trying to get the policy changed);
6) Procedural agreement (he thinks that the processes by which the TPS report policies and practices were established are fair and legitimate, and believes that his concerns about the practices could be heard);
7) Ideal normative agreement (he believes the TPS report policies are genuinely reasonable and effective, and would follow them regardless of punishment or reward or who was requesting them).[3]

These forms of compliance-gaining can be loosely categorized into three: unthinking obedience, coercion, legitimacy. Motives 1–3 are forms of blind obedience; 4 and 5 are forms of coercion (punishment/reward); 6 and 7 are in the category of legitimacy. In terms of getting a group that can quickly shift to new forms of behavior without much cost, coercion and legitimacy are very common forms of compliance-gaining, but they have their limits.

Coercion is often effective, but only if threats of punishment are plausible. For the threats to be plausible, there must exist significant structures of surveillance—Chester either has to believe it's likely that he will get found out if he doesn't follow the practices, or else the punishment has to be so severe that he isn't willing to take the chance. Similarly, if he's only following the rules because of expected rewards, he has to believe that someone will notice if he does the reports, and the rewards have to be high enough to overcome any aversion he has, and make up for opportunity cost (that is, instead of doing the reports, he might do something that would make him even more money, such as selling office supplies out of the back of a truck). So, the company has to have a person who checks to see that all the reports are done correctly, and that takes time and money. And the company will also have to fire people from time to time, or else the threats aren't plausible (and therefore not motivating), and firing people isn't cheap. Rewards, similarly, take supervision, and they cost.

If we shift the analogy to a community and to trying to gain compliance to some rules (paying taxes, stopping at stop signs) we have the same problems—there is a cost to making sure people are following the rules, enacting the punishments, rewarding compliance. Coercion is expensive.

Legitimacy doesn't have costs of surveillance and punishment, and it's tremendously effective, but it's slow. It only works in a realm of argumentation, in which dissent is treated as an honorable practice—if dissent is routinely silenced, then there isn't legitimacy. Deliberation takes time, and no one ends up with exactly what they want—there is always compromise. The argument for deliberation is that, if, for example, the TPS reports and formats are a waste of time, deliberation will expose that fact, and the company might end up with a different and much more efficient policy.

On the other hand, each new person who comes on board will have to be *persuaded*, through legitimate argumentation, that the TPS reports are useful and necessary, so there is an endless legitimation process. There is no need for the surveillance, punishment, or reward practices, so those costs are non-existent, but there is instead the cost of argumentation, and that's a significant cost in terms of time and intellectual commitment—in systems of legitimacy, change tends to be slow because it relies on an inclusive rhetoric of argumentation.

If people follow the protocols out of blind obedience, however, there is no cost of argumentation or surveillance. If Chester follows the TPS rules out of loyalty to traditions or rituals of the tribe, then enforcement of the rules is both internalized (if he breaks protocol, he will feel disloyal to the tribe) and diffusively externalized (other members of the tribe will scold him, or, if he persists, they will shun or otherwise socially punish him). Tradition, then, is an effective and cost-efficient way to get compliance.

The problem with tradition (and also its virtue) is that change to any practice is slow—at least as slow as it is in systems grounded in legitimacy. People don't want to give up old practices, and it takes a long time for new practices to gain the status of tradition/ritual.

Blind obedience does not have to be strictly to the traditions of the tribe. Blind obedience can also be to membership in the tribe and deference to its leader. In situations in which the "tradition" of the tribe is blind obedience to the leader and his[4] spokespeople (those who announce/model what the new beliefs, practices, and talking points are), then there is the diffused enforcement of tribal loyalty, but also the possibility of immediate changes: if the leader to whom one is perfectly obedient announces a change of course, then loyalty is demonstrated through unquestioningly making that change.

And *that* is charismatic leadership.

Charismatic Leadership and Authoritarianism

Charismatic leadership, as Max Weber and other sociologists theorize it, is not something a leader does or is (a leader with charisma), but a source of power for the leader that comes from the kind of relationship he can create with people who see themselves as represented by that leader.[5] In that kind of relationship, the leader is sublime, beyond anything negative, a pure expression of the true identity of the followers. This is what rhetoricians have termed "ultimate identification." Followers have an unmediated relationship with the leader, so he doesn't lead them—he *is* them in a position of leadership.

Political scientist Ann Ruth Willner describes the four characteristics of charismatic leadership as such: followers perceive the leader as "superhuman," they "follow blindly," they "unconditionally comply," and they "give unqualified emotional commitment."[6]

Charismatic authority says a policy is good or a claim is true because it's made by *this* person. In a charismatic authority relationship, dissent from that person's decisions is impossible because it necessarily implies that the leader is not a person with perfect judgment, and rational dissent is even less likely because the whole relationship is grounded in irrational personal commitment.

Willner describes this kind of relationship between leader and follower in ways that make it clear why this model is so attractive to people who are thinking about getting Chester to do his TPS reports quickly, often, and thoroughly:

> The followers abdicate judgment to the leader. Belief and obedience are almost automatic. Followers accept and believe that the past was as the leader portrays it, that the present is as he depicts it, and that the future will be as he predicts it. And they follow without hesitation his prescriptions for action.[7]

If an organization can create a cult-like level of commitment to the organization, its mission, and its actions, then it will have none of the costs (in terms of time or money) associated with coercive or legitimate methods of authority.

Business paeans to charismatic leadership are legion, but they dance around the fact that they are actually calling for transforming businesses into authoritarian cults. As leadership and management scholars Bruce Avolio and Francis Yammerino summarize it, leaders with that kind of relationship to followers "foster performance beyond expected standards by developing an emotional attachment with followers and other leaders, which is tied to a common cause, which contributes to the 'greater good' or larger collective."[8]

Here is the problem: Avolio and Yammerino have hidden their whole argument in that criterion of "a common cause that contributes to the greater good." This criterion enables advocates of charismatic leadership to dodge any disconfirming examples by engaging in what rhetoricians call the "No true

Scotsman" move—basically, disconfirming examples are simply not counted as "true" examples. That is, charismatic leaders do good for their organizations, period, and any charismatic leader who doesn't do good isn't truly a charismatic leader.

What that move ignores is that a major problem with charismatic leadership—and why it's so bad for democracy—is that the relationship itself allows propaganda about the end goals of the organization (in fact, promotes it) but prohibits debate about those ends. In a relationship of charismatic authority, criticizing the leader is impossible because the whole point of relying on that person's decision-making ability is that there is no standard to which you might appeal other than his judgment. If he has come to a judgment, that judgment is, by definition, just.

Charismatic leadership only consistently leads to good community decisions if the leader is magically endowed with better judgment than everyone else in the community (precisely the myth that powers charismatic leadership). The myth is that his judgment is *so* good, in fact, that he doesn't need to hear anyone else's point of view—he has a supernatural ability to see every issue from every perspective. If an organization doesn't have a leader with a supernatural ability to make the right choices about end goals every time, then charismatic leadership will enable the leader to take the organization to the wrong ends that much more effectively.

After all, if followers' commitment to the leader's vision is emotional, then they are not expected to think critically about whether the leader is taking the community in the right direction—they are to follow.

Historians of authoritarianism and genocide are deeply aware of the dangers of charismatic leadership. For instance, Ian Kershaw's *Fateful Choices* is an extraordinary book showing how Japan's Emperor Hirohito, Italy's Benito Mussolini, and Germany's Adolf Hitler all made disastrously bad decisions in 1940–41 that looked good in the moment given the information and priorities they had.[9] Hirohito, for instance, was by definition in a charismatic leadership position with the public, and Kershaw argues that he decided to declare war on the US because he was surrounded by optimists who wouldn't (perhaps couldn't) doubt that Hirohito's end goals (an Asian empire led by Japan) were anything other than good and wise. The highly charismatic Mussolini was likewise supported and encouraged in his disastrous decision to invade Greece by advisors who shared his end goals. And the amazing book *Hitler and His Generals* shows that Hitler's military decisions couldn't be doubted by his generals, even when (as in his decisions about Stalingrad) they were disastrous.[10] These leaders all had the wrong priorities, and they were getting bad information *because* they were surrounded by people who treated dissent as disloyalty and who insisted the right course of action was obvious.[11]

What these historians of authoritarianism, as well as some of the more critical writers about business, recognize is that because charismatic leaders can get followers to act quickly, passionately, and without a second thought, they can lead those followers right off a cliff. And they have.

Although authors in business suggest charismatic leadership should involve the leader behaving ethically, what they often ignore is a lesson that historians have learned well—organizations and states that let charismatic leadership lead them off a cliff were following leaders who sincerely believed they were "behaving ethically." Hitler sincerely believed that a world dominated by Germany, and a Germany cleansed of the genetically "weak," was a good thing. Disgraced former CEO of Enron and charismatic leader, Kenneth Lay, said and probably sincerely believed that his actions were based on a desire to look out for the best interest of his stockholders and employees.

I'm not saying that Hitler and Lay were right, obviously, nor am I advocating some kind of moral relativism. I'm saying that individuals are not very good judges of their own motives, and that charismatic leadership is therefore profoundly dangerous because it keeps leaders out of the kind of system that ensures they have to hear disconfirming evidence—that is, arguments that their goals might not be good.

In business schools, charismatic leadership is praised because it motivates followers to go above and beyond; followers who believe in the leader are less likely to resist. And, while that might seem like an unequivocal good, it's only good if the leader is leading the institution in a good direction. If the direction is bad, then disaster just happens faster.

Charismatic leadership is a relationship that requires complete acquiescence and submission on the part of the followers. It is a relationship of pure hierarchy, simultaneously robust and fragile, because it can withstand an extraordinary amount of disconfirming evidence (that the leader is not actually all that good, does not have the requisite traits, is out of her depth, is making bad decisions) by simply rejecting them; it is fragile, however, insofar as the admission of a serious flaw on the part of the leader destroys the relationship entirely. A leader who relies on legitimacy isn't weakened by disagreement (and might even be strengthened by it), but a charismatic leader is.

So, the obvious solution is for followers to be vigilant and disagree when the charismatic leader is headed in the wrong direction. But how do followers know if a charismatic leader is following bad policies? They don't. They can't. That the leader appears to be following risky and unwise policies actually enhances his position as a charismatic leader, and calls on followers to demonstrate their commitment to him by continuing to believe him despite his engaging in policies all the experts say is wrong, that contradict what he said he'd do, and that might seem ill-considered. Followers must like that the charismatic leader is playing from the gut.

Once someone has entered in the charismatic leadership relationship, there is no way to admit that the leader is flawed without the follower(s) admitting to themselves that they are flawed judges of character. Charismatic leadership is inherently toxic in that it connects the followers' sense of self-worth to the possibly arbitrary policy agenda of the person they have decided really represents them.

Trump's Charismatic Leadership

Communities in which charismatic leadership is the dominant relationship between voters and a leader don't generally end well. When there is a single leader who is mastering all the available energy, such communities usually end up in an unnecessary war (for example, the Sicilian Expedition, Napoleonic wars, or WWII). If it is a situation with a lot of rhetors—that is, speakers, including pundits, cultural commentators, or political operatives—involved in drawing power from the charismatic leadership relationship, the result might be a tremendous cultural commitment to an obviously unwise policy (such as the US commitment to slavery and, later, segregation, or current homophobic policies).

Trump is in the former category. He is not a person to give up power, and he doesn't play well with others (and that's what his base likes about him). He has already shown that he will enact policies that harm his base, and they have shown they don't care. This isn't about some kind of rational commitment on their part to his policy agenda. This isn't about policies at all—it is about being on the winning side.

The strongest evidence for this point is Trump supporters' repeated tendency to respond to claims about Trump doing something wrong by claiming that Democrats did the same thing. It's an interestingly irrational argument. For instance, when Trump fired FBI Director James Comey (and said he did so because Comey was pursuing the Russia investigation),[12] the pro-Trump propaganda machine pointed to examples of Democrats, especially President Obama and Hillary Clinton, firing high-level officials. Their point may have been factually true, but their point is also completely irrelevant to whether Trump did something wrong or not. It does not matter if Obama or Clinton engaged in human sacrifice at every full moon and therefore fired someone. Clinton might have kicked puppies and fired the vice president, and that's actually irrelevant to whether Trump fired Comey because Comey was going to expose Trump's reliance on Russia having interfered with the election. Both can be true. But Trump supporters don't see that "DEMS DID IT, TOO!" doesn't answer the question about Trump's bad decisions at all.

In a charismatic leadership relationship, the followers don't care if their leader did something bad; they only care whether (in some weird calculus in their minds) their leader can be positioned as better than the other. For people engaged in a charismatic leadership relationship with Trump, the question (every question) is an opportunity to prove that Trump is better than others, and so any bad (even if irrelevant) action on the part of the others is proof that Trump is actually good.

In short, charismatic leadership/authority is *essentially* authoritarian, and *essentially* hostile to democratic deliberation, which involves disagreement, argument, legitimacy, and compromise. Right now, for various reasons, we have a toxic combination of talking points in business, in lay theories of politics, and in for-profit media that glorify charismatic leadership because of its efficiency in both speed and (supposed) lack of cost. As a result, large numbers of people in our democracy believe that charismatic leadership is the most effective form of leadership in business, that the problem with government is that it is preserved from the market (so it should be more like business), and that we just need to elect someone who will cut through the bullshit and do what's obviously right.

Whether we should make government run more like business is a complicated claim, but it is not complicated if we think businesses should be run on the basis of charismatic leadership. The argument for charismatic leadership in government is a straightforward argument for abandoning democracy in favor of authoritarianism.

Conclusion

I began this essay with the fomented outrage over Julius Caesar looking like Trump. That outrage wasn't the consequence of an informed understanding of why a comparison to Shakespeare's Caesar might be insulting—it actually isn't. In charismatic leadership, followers so emotionally identify with the leader such that seeing their leader killed makes themselves feel physically attacked. For Trump supporters who were outraged by Shakespeare in the Park, it doesn't matter what Shakespeare did or didn't mean. What matters is their pure identification with the leader.

As I said at the beginning, Shakespeare's treatment of Caesar is complicated, largely because Shakespeare was deeply ambivalent about what we would now consider democratic discourse (look at how quickly Marc Antony turns the crowd, or how difficult it is for Coriolanus to maintain popular approval). But Shakespeare wasn't ambivalent about leaders who insist on hyperbolic displays of personal loyalty. They are the source of tragedy.

The truly Shakespearean moment in Trump's administration in the summer of 2017, around that same time as the Shakespeare in the Park controversy, was a cabinet meeting at which Trump asked high-level members of his administration for declarations of loyalty to him. And anyone even a little familiar with Shakespeare immediately thought of the scene in *King Lear* when Lear demands professions of loyalty. Trump isn't Caesar; he's Lear. Lear demanded oaths of blind loyalty, and, as often happens under those circumstances, the person who was committed to the truth wouldn't take such an oath. In *King Lear*, that person was the hero.

Notes

1   Stephanie Nolasco, "Sponsors Flee New York City Theater Company over Trump-killing Scene," *FoxNews.com*, June 12, 2017, http://www.foxnews.com/entertainment/2017/06/12/sponsors-flee-new-york-city-theater-company-over-trump-killing-scene.html.

2   Kenneth Burke, *Rhetoric of Motives* (Berkeley, CA: University of California Press, 1969), 21.

3   For more on this chart, see David Held, *Models of Democracy* (Palo Alto, CA: Stanford University Press, 2006).

4   At least in the current moment, charismatic leaders are usually "he."

5   See Max Weber, "The Three Types of Legitimate Rule," *Berkeley Publications in Society and Institutions*, 4.1 (1958): 1–11.

6   Ann Ruth Willner, *The Spellbinders: Charismatic Political Leadership* (New Haven, CT: Yale University Press, 1985), 8.

7   Willner, *The Spellbinders*, 7.

8   Bruce J. Avolio and Francis J. Yammarino, eds., *Transformational and Charismatic Leadership: The Road Ahead 10th Anniversary Edition* (Bingley, UK: Emerald Group Publishing Limited, 2013), xvii.

9   Ian Kershaw, *Fateful Choices: Ten Decisions That Changed the World, 1940–1941* (New York: Penguin Books, 2008).

10 Helmut Heiber and David M. Glantz, eds., *Hitler and His Generals: Military Conferences, 1942–1945* (New York: Enigma Books, 2002).

11 It is interesting to note that, even in 1944, or even among soldiers encircled at Stalingrad, there were people who insisted that Hitler had been right all along, but he had been misled by his advisors — they were in a charismatic leadership relationship, and they could not admit that they'd put their trust in the wrong person.

12 Ali Vitali and Corky Siemaszko, "Trump Interview with Lester Holt: President Asked Comey If He Was Under Investigation," *NBC News*, May 11, 2017, https://www.nbcnews.com/news/us-news/trump-reveals-he-asked-comey-whether-he-was-under-investigation-n757821.

Paul J. Achter

Great Television: Trump and the Shadow Archetype

I did not want to write about Donald Trump. But my resistance decreased after listening to my kids talk about him on our commute to their school. It's interesting when elementary-aged children talk about Trump because he violates so many of the basic values we try to teach them. Be kind, don't lie, treat everyone with respect—Trump does the opposite of almost all of the values we teach young kids. When our pastor gave a sermon about forgiveness and asked us to think about a person we did not agree with so that we could try to understand, my eight-year-old thought about Donald Trump. Though I was initially surprised that my kids paid attention to or cared about the presidency, a study by the Harvard Shorenstein Center showed that, in his first 100 days as president, Trump was the topic of 41 percent of national news coverage, three times the coverage presidents usually receive during that time period.[1] I realize now that nothing will keep them from hearing about President Trump, and that very little he does matches what they are learning.

Trump supporters often value in him the same things my children find confusing and wrong. Supporters like him because he "says what's on his mind" and doesn't try to be "politically correct." They laud him as a "disruption" to the usual order. Trump says the things that his supporters want to say, but cannot say because those things should not be said in public, giving voice to white racism, sexism, to fear and hatred of "radical Islamist terrorism," to contempt for the poor. He violates norms of civility while holding perhaps the world's biggest megaphone.

What's troubling is that his style may increase his visibility, especially on television. Not since Reagan has a president been so associated with television and so understood in terms of television. Why? Trump's ascendance raises questions about historical expectations for the presidency and about the ability of news organizations to protect democratic values.

Archetypes on Television

Trump is extremely self-conscious about how he is represented on TV. His presidency has met with fascination and high TV ratings. At the "big three" cable channels, MSNBC, Fox, and CNN, combined audiences are up 33 percent since 2016, and he is one main reason.[2]

Trump does not regularly use a computer, but his tweets are often driven by TV, and, by all accounts, he could not live a day without it. He reads and watches stories about himself, sending journalists feedback, calling TV shows, and always trying to influence coverage. His staff delivers screenshots of his TV coverage to him after major events so he can see how he looks and what chyrons are paired with what images.[3] Although he cannot control the way he is represented, he is more invested than ever in trying. He has studied the news cycle like a public relations specialist:

> One of the things I've learned about the press is that they're always hungry for a good story, and the more sensational the better... The point is that if you are a little outrageous, or if you do things that are bold or controversial, the press is going to write about you... That's why a little hyperbole never hurts. I play to people's fantasies... people want to believe that something is the biggest and the greatest and the most spectacular. I call it truthful hyperbole. It's an innocent form of exaggeration — and a very effective form of promotion.[4]

Presidents are always subjects of outsized media attention, with cameras and eyes trained on them any time they are in public and any time they wish for publicity. But in seeking media attention and monitoring his coverage, President Trump is unique. He has internalized the logics of television, so much that it's difficult to understand Trump without talking about television.

Trump has attempted to shape his character as a heroic capitalist, stern father-leader, and an expert doer of deals, but he has moved between hero and villain many times over the decades. In TV and literary terms, Trump is a shadow figure, a representative of our cultural unconscious, the unspoken "true spirit" of life, a character whose actions offer constant contrasts to the thoughtful and democratic people we profess to be.

As president, he occupies the space of the shadow — exaggerating, lying, and breaking rules once thought to be unassailable in politics — and earning disapproval numbers higher than any other president in history. At the same time, his businesses and wealth make him a hero. A reality TV character can and must be fluid, moving back and forth "between the pariah and the icon, the hated and the wor-shipped,"[5] because, loved or hated, the dramatic potential of a figure is the common currency of television drama.

TV features many archetypal characters — heroes, villains, tricksters — that have evolved over time in film, literature, and other narrative forms of popular culture. They reappear because they reflect and constitute a particular culture, reinforcing audience values as they shape and reshape them. For audiences, archetypal characters come bearing lessons about the values a culture holds to be important, about who we are and who we want to be as a people, about how we might act as we navigate life. Trump is a central character in everyday news discourse in an era in which the distinction between reality TV and news TV seems to have dissolved.[6] Trump is a shadow character, that is, partly because of his interest in and use of television, which shapes the way he is represented in media.

Rhetoric, Representation, and Archetype

Given Trump's unrestrained behavior, people—including people in the media—often accuse him of using rhetoric. When we talk about rhetoric today we often think about persuasion, and, most often, dishonest persuasion. Trump's lies and exaggerations leave him open to becoming another example in a line of abusers of the art, a person whose focus on the persuasive effects of his words comes at the expense of ethics.

Analyzing Trump's rhetoric is important, but words, images, and other symbols have functions that include—but are more than—persuasion. What we call rhetoric includes words and images *about* Trump—in other words, media representations of Trump—and that means the acts of characterizing him matter. The everyday work of the press and of television personalities as they describe him for audiences is very important.

A description of Trump is rhetorical in that the very labels used are imbued with values and thus constitute him in our mind's eye (Trump prefers "billionaire" and "real estate magnate" to describe himself, for example). The point of a rhetorical analysis like this is not to determine the "truth" of who Trump is, but, rather, to understand how Trump is talked about and to think about what the implications are of such talk. Rhetoric about Trump associates him with TV frequently, and associating him with TV and plotting him in stories about TV is a fundamental act of rhetoric that is often overlooked.

Put another way, in the contemporary mediated world, presidents and other public figures are *constituted* by the pervasive language and imagery of news journalism. This does not mean that their material, physical existence is irrelevant. It means that their physical existence only has meaning to audiences insofar as language and images communicate about them. If rhetoric about Trump did not matter, Trump would not study his coverage so closely and he would not call news organizations "fake news" every time he disagrees with something said about him. Few of us will encounter a president first hand, but nearly all of us regularly encounter stories about presidents, whether online, on TV, on the radio, or in another form.

By circulating such representations, journalism serves important audience needs. News stories suggest proper courses of action, they teach us how to navigate relationships, they offer ways of thinking about history, they praise the good and vilify the bad. The characters in the news offer audiences points of identification that make stories easy to understand. My kids know about Trump because he is a central character in a news story every day who gives us a way to talk about how to behave.

Trump as TV Viewer

Any parent today will tell you that raising a child means thinking about how much "screen time" that child has. As a parent, I am inundated with messages about how much TV my kids should watch, how much time they can spend on a phone or tablet or computer. Few of these messages are encouraging — most instill the fear that too much screen time is a bad thing. Many articles are written as if screen time is a zero-sum experience and that every second in front of a screen is time a child should have spent outside playing or reading a book. Many messages about TV and kids proceed without specifically identifying what is on the screen, flattening the differences between a child learning math on an iPad and one playing *Call of Duty* on an Xbox. We set limits on "screen time." We brag about not watching TV and refusing to let our kids watch TV as a way to demonstrate our participation in higher forms of culture. We define TV as the opposite of books, as surface and not depth, entertainment and not seriousness. Rhetoric about the amount of screen time and the type of content children interact with on screens talks about screens like sugar — as something parents should let their children enjoy only in moderation.

When I teach a TV criticism course and ask my students to talk about shows they watch, they always respond with some level of shame, whether it is related to which shows they watch or how much they watch. TV's "low culture" status is reflected in higher education curricula, where departments of media studies are dwarfed by departments of English and History. TV may be the storytelling center of culture, but it is a guilty pleasure.

Articles that detail how much TV Trump watches are now commonplace. *The Washington Post, The Atlantic, Fortune,* and numerous other outlets have analyzed Trump's "TV diet," concluding that he watches around five hours of television per day, comparing him unfavorably to previous presidents, and quoting experts who say his TV habits are an unpresidential "obsession" and a poor use of time.[7] In a story titled "The unbreakable bond between Trump and his television remote," MSNBC concluded that "it can't be healthy" that Trump turns to TV for foreign policy guidance, watches every day from roughly 6:30–9 a.m., and uses the same language of political TV shows in tweets and speeches.[8] A *Politico* story about Trump's media habits revealed that staff were "not able to wean him off" TV because he "gets bored and likes to watch" at all hours of the day.[9] Another journalist compared the attempts by his White House staff to keep Trump from watching TV to his own efforts to keep his toddler from watching too much TV.[10] Like lots of children, Trump loves television and those around him think it's a dangerous habit.

TV viewing is a central part of Trump's shadow character and his interest in TV is apparently comprehensive. Colleagues reportedly use TV appearances to communicate with him because they know he might be watching. He watches how his team and journalists talk about him, he texts and calls TV personalities and surrogates during appearance. His first press secretary, Sean Spicer, was by most measures doing a poor job, but before firing him Trump defended Spicer's ratings as the metric by which the press secretary should be judged.[11]

Characterizations of Trump as a person who loves to watch TV carry with them an implicit criticism that Trump is not up to the job—as signs that he lacks intelligence, disdains nuance, and is dangerously averse to deep explanation. The presidency is associated with speech and the written word, with nuance and "high culture." But reporter Mike Allen says Trump is "not a book guy: In fact, some advisers say they don't recall seeing him read one or even talking about one beyond his own, *The Art of the Deal*."[12] We hear that his closest advisors try to keep him away from TV and numerous critics argue that Trump lacks an appropriate "attention span" for the job. Reports about a May 2017 trip to Saudi Arabia indicated that foreign leaders were asked to keep their speeches short and to pepper their written materials with Trump's name because he pays attention most to where his name appears.

Characterizing Trump as a TV-obsessed child, however, obscures the feedback loop at work and how stories about Trump's TV habits support the TV industry. Programs that Trump watches and talks about can hike their ad rates, and producers now make programming choices knowing that he might be watching and tweeting.[13] When he singles out CNN or *Morning Joe* for abuse it *makes news*, and it does not necessarily hurt the targets of his ire.[14] MSNBC President Phil Griffin told *The Hill* he wished Trump complained about MSNBC "because it's like a promo for CNN all the time."[15]

Trump as TV Character

Trump's shadow archetype—his characterization as a bigoted, TV-obsessed lightweight—is proving irresistible for cable news. Like the anti-hero of fictional dramas, the typically male character who is celebrated for rule-breaking, the shadow character is immoral and impulsive but attractive to audiences. Much as viewers binged on the story of a cancer-stricken chemistry teacher who mastered the production of crystal methamphetamine on *Breaking Bad*, Trumpism draws audiences. He is a character in a story that is personal, dark, novel, dramatic, and full of conflict. Defending his choice to hire staffers Trump had fired during the campaign, CNN President Jeff Zucker said he made the choice because fired Trump staffers were "characters in a drama." "Zucker surely knew that his hiring of Corey Lewandowski (Trump's former campaign manager) would create controversy and in turn give his anchors something to talk about," wrote Jonathan Mahler. And "that is exactly what happened: The hiring became a cable-news story about cable news."[16] Zucker viewed CNN as *part* of the story of Trump, not merely an entity reporting *about* Trump.

One purpose of rhetoric about Trump's TV habits, then, is to undermine his credibility as an intellectual, thinking person. But such rhetoric also promotes the shows and networks he's most passionate about, whether he likes them or not. It is "earned media" attention for the networks that identifies news organizations as characters in a drama with Trump. It grants free publicity to an enormous audience.

Since Trump secured the GOP nomination in the summer of 2016, ratings at CNN, MSNBC, and Fox have all risen. In 2016 CNN reported that it made $100 million more than it had the previous fiscal year. Referring to Trump, an advertising executive from Anheuser Busch told NPR that the presidential campaign really "popped" and that it "was a fun one to watch."[17] "Trump really pops" is the kind of thing we say about a red vase in a beige room. In regards to television, it's an argument about ratings, which influence how much news organizations can charge for advertisements. As the *New York Times* wrote, Trump is "a human breaking-news event," a figure who seemed as if he "had built his entire campaign around nothing so much as his singular ability to fill cable news's endless demand for engaging content."[18]

Never mind that "engaging content" means explicit sexism and racism. As former GOP Senator and Trump surrogate Newt Gingrich observed, Trump "is very attuned to the fact that cable networks have 24 hours a day that they need to fill— and if you're interesting, you are gold."[19] It has become cliché to observe that Trump's presidency is "a reality show" and that he only "plays president" on TV.[20] Trump, so goes the argument, is an "interesting" and "engaging" TV character on a drama that uses the presidency as a vehicle—a point borne out by frequent stories that compare his presidency to the political drama *House of Cards.*

For media organizations, then, Trump's shadow performance is an opportunity. "Official Washington and the press corps may mostly despise the president," wrote a Fox News columnist, "but they love how easy he makes their jobs."[21] The same can be said for media buyers, who determine how networks spend their advertising money, and who now realize "that it's hard to beat real-world politics for intrigue and suspense."[22] Career politicians, by contrast, find that Trump makes their job harder. According to one GOP consultant, Republicans don't understand Trump "because he's a creature of television and they're creatures of politics. They care about the details, he cares about what's on TV... and they have to navigate around it."[23]

To be sure, Trump's embrace of TV values has not made for a smooth, efficient presidency. Following the logics of public relations and television, the Trump administration seems to see all of its problems "as a failure out of the communications office to sell the administration's story," as if being aggressive and attacking critics harshly "can change broad-ranging criminal probes."[24] Being a villain on TV neither solves political problems nor does it completely diminish a president's power.

Nevertheless, like all archetypes, the shadow character tells us something about the audience that follows it. Trump's "bad" shadow reveals our nation's white racism, sexism, and fear of terrorism. He gives voice to barely concealed undercurrents that have been a part of American life for a long time. He amplifies the neo-Confederate, anti-Obama energy that manifested in the beginnings of the Tea Party movement in 2009. He revives an early Bush-era rhetoric of terrorism that characterizes Muslims and Arab people in the narrow terminology of "us and them."

But it is not sufficient to say that a shadow is a reflection *only* of a society's bad impulses. Writing about the function of shadows in photography, rhetoric scholar Robert Hariman points out that "Shadows... might reveal one's sins, but that might be more melodramatic than is needed much of the time. A shadow also could lend itself to recollection or prophecy or other opportunities for reflection."[25] A shadow also reflects a culture's ambivalence and emerging values.

Consider the following. During the Republican National Convention, Trump called surrogate Jeffrey Lord while he was on CNN talking to Anderson Cooper—itself remarkable—to complain about CNN's coverage of his candidacy. Lord then relayed the complaints to Cooper. When Lord later told him the story, CNN's Jeff Zucker grabbed him by the lapels of his suit coat and said "That is great television!"[26]

Less obviously, then, Trump's shadow reveals the triumph of news market values as American virtues. TV-loving Trump is a character in a drama that *includes* CNN, one who embodies and amplifies the neoliberal logics of for-profit news organizations—of conflict and incivility in the name of ratings and revenue. In Zucker's view, there's no reason not to serve viewers more of the topic that interests them—this is what news channels do. Trump is good for cable news, Zucker told *Variety* magazine, and "there is no evidence that the interest in him is waning in any way."[27] Speaking to the *New York Times*, Zucker similarly noted, "I have always been interested in the news, but I've always been interested in what's popular... I've always had a little bit of a populist take on things." The Trump presidency, he says, is "the biggest story we could ever imagine."[28] Story, character, popularity—these are the CNN President's words. As cable news organizations celebrate their achievements, the metric that matters most is audiences and ratings.

Hero or villain, Trump draws viewers and clicks, and that is both his goal and the goal of cable TV news. This synergy between candidate and medium is not entirely new in politics, but its evolution via Trump is worthy of attention. As pundits and journalists rightly agonize about political partisanship, divisiveness, and party identification, our "other" selves manifest in our shadow character president—our default veneration of wealth and the wealthy, our cultural belief that earning money or simply possessing money is a good thing, a belief that earnings justify the means of earning. As Steven Marche writes, "Trump is not imposing distortion on American voters. He's just catching up with the marketplace. A people of screens will inevitably choose screened people to lead them."[29] In the presidential election of 2016, Trump won, and so did the morality of the screen.

It's a far cry from the beginnings of TV news, when the Fairness Doctrine and the "equal time" rule required news stations to make attempts to balance their coverage of politics and to offer contrasting views on controversial issues. Those rules were designed to align TV news toward the public good, and while the spirit of them remains in how people talk about news, even Fox News has stopped using its "Fair and Balanced" slogan.

TV and American Values: A Conclusion

Rhetoricians, media critics, and political economists have always argued that it's impossible for news organizations to act as observers from a position "outside" politics. News organizations *create* and *participate* in dramas about politics. What is interesting is that executives from MSNBC and CNN are saying publicly that Trump is a TV character in a story for the ages that they are riding to profit. The first TV networks were all dependent upon the government for access to public airwaves, and for that reason, for decades the FCC sought to make broadcasters accountable to the public and to democratic values. The success of cable channels has changed the equation. As Brian Beutler argued, "The press is not a pro-democracy trade, it is a pro-media trade. By and large, it doesn't act as a guardian of civic norms and liberal institutions—except when press freedoms and access itself are at stake."[30]

It should go without saying that the presidency is an incredibly important job and that most Americans value it, too. As I have argued here, the rhetoric surrounding Trump that associates him with television often does so as a way to imply that he is unfit for the job. Without a doubt, we ought to be concerned that credible political observers think of him as a lightweight who only "plays president" on TV. There is far too much at stake. Likewise, my children and a legion of critics are right to point out that Trump violates the values of respect, fairness, and kindness.

American values are not always so straightforward, however. Stories about Trump's love of television and his persona as a "politically incorrect" shadow character underscore the ability of the news to vilify the president while enthralling audiences endlessly. Without news stories, most of us would never know about him. Trump's fascination with television is surpassed perhaps only by the industry's fascination with him.

As such, Trump's presidency raises the concern that future politicians can similarly "disrupt" political norms of behavior in undemocratic ways, and that the news media will be powerless to stop it because the drama is irresistible. This is not an argument that rhetoric about Trump and TV prove that ratings drive *everything*. The same exposure that gives Trump name-recognition and constant attention forms the foundation of resistant acts against him. Not all publicity is good publicity, and his future in politics and business is uncertain.

That said, Americans are primed to underestimate the shadow of the market. The banking and finance industry crashed the American economy a decade ago and we seem to have barely noticed — much less sent people to prison. We watch upwardly-mobile home shows about houses we could never afford. We shower attention on people who are rich for simply being rich.

The news networks and shows may deny that they are aligned with any political party, but they share with Trump the ideology of the marketplace, where making money is the goal. That is their purpose, and there is no reason to think that it will serve the needs of the American people.

Notes

1   Thomas E. Patterson, "News Coverage of Donald Trump's First 100

Days," *Harvard Shorenstein Center*, May 18, 2017, https://shorenstein
center.org/news-coverage-donald-trumps-first-100-days/.

2 Joe Otterson, "Cable News Ratings: Fox News Breaks Records, MSNBC
Posts Significant Growth," *Variety*, March 28, 2017, http://variety.com/
2017/tv/news/cable-news-ratings-fox-news-msnbc-1202017940/.

3 Chris Cillizza, "Donald Trump Is WAY More Obsessed with Cable TV
Than You Even Think," *CNN.com*, August 9, 2017, http://www.cnn.
com/2017/08/09/politics/trump-tv-chyrons/index.html.

4 Donald J. Trump, *The Art of the Deal* (New York: Random House, 2009),
quoted in Timothy O'Brien, *TrumpNation: The Art of Being the Donald*
(New York: Warner Books, 2005), 98.

5 Stephen Marche, "Celebrity Warfare: Image and Politics in the Age of
Trump," *Los Angeles Review of Books*, May 23, 2017, https://lareviewof
books.org/article/celebrity-warfare-image-politics-age-trump/.

6 Marche, "Celebrity Warfare."

7 Elaine Godfrey, "Trump's TV Obsession Is a First," *The Atlantic*, April 3,
2017, https://www.theatlantic.com/politics/archive/2017/04/donald-
trump- americas-first-tv-president/521640/.

8 Steve Benen, "The Unbreakable Bond between Trump and His Television Remote," *MSNBC.com*, January 26, 2017, http://www.msnbc.
com/rachel-maddow-show/the-unbreakable-bond-between-trump-
and-his-television-remote.

9 Phillip Bump, "A Visual Guide to Donald Trump's Media Habits,"
Washington Post, January 24, 2017, https://www.washingtonpost.com/
news/politics/wp/2017/01/24/a-visual-guide-to-donald-trumps-
media-habits/?utm_term=.94c1a717f6c3.

10 Matthew Yglesias "Trump's Advisers Say They Can't Stop Him from
Watching Too Much Television," *Vox.com*, June 8, 2017, https://www.
vox.com/2017/6/8/15761726/trump-watching-comey.

11 Ashley Parker, "Inside Trump's Obsession with Cable TV," *Washington
Post*, April 23, 2017, https://www.washingtonpost.com/politics/
everyone-tunes-in-inside-trumps-obsession-with-cable-tv/2017/04/
23/3c52bd6c-25e3-11e7-a1b3-faff0034e2de_story.html.

12 Mike Allen and Jim VandeHei, "Trump 101: What He Reads and
Watches," *Axios*, January 24, 2017, https://www.axios.com/trump-101-
what-he-reads-and-watches-2210510272.html.

13 Daniel Lippman and Anna Palmer, "TV Networks Hiking Ad Rates for
Shows Trump Watches," *Politico*, February 4, 2017, http://www.
politico.com/story/2017/02/trump-tv-ad-rates-morning-joe-oreilly-
234647; Steven Perlberg, "How Donald Trump Launched a New
Golden Age For Cable TV," *BuzzFeed*, February 14, 2017, https://www.
buzzfeed.com/stevenperlberg/how-donald-trump-launched-a-new-
golden-age-for-cable-tv.

14 Craig Fitzpatrick, "CNN Predicts Record Profits Thanks to Trump,"
Newstalk, February 17, 2017, http://www.newstalk.com/CNN-profits-

up-thanks-to-Trump.

[15] Joe Concha, "MSNBC President: Ratings on Rise Because We Give 'Smartest Coverage Out There,'" *The Hill*, March 2, 2017, http://thehill. com/homenews/media/322003-msnbc-president-ratings-on-rise-because-we-give-smartest-coverage-out-there.

[16] Jonathan Mahler, "CNN Had a Problem. Donald Trump Solved It," *New York Times*, April 4, 2017, https://www.nytimes.com/2017/04/04/magazine/cnn-had-a-problem-donald-trump-solved-it.html.

[17] David Folkenflick, "AT&T Deal For Time Warner Casts Renewed Attention On CNN," *NPR*, October 25, 2016, http://www.npr.org/2016/10/25/499299869/at-t-deal-for-time-warner-casts-renewed-attention-on-cnn.

[18] Mahler, "CNN Had a Problem."

[19] Parker, "Inside Trump's Obsession with Cable TV."

[20] Jennifer Rubin, "Trump's Not Really President—He Just Plays One on TV," *Washington Post*, July 31, 2017, https://www.washingtonpost.com/blogs/right-turn/wp/2017/07/31/trumps-not-really-president-he-just-plays-one-on-tv/?utm_term=.4c1f4738a6e9; Callum Borchers, "Trump Is Turning His Paris Climate Decision Into a Television Event," *Washington Post*, June 1, 2017, https://www.washingtonpost.com/news/the-fix/wp/2017/06/01/trump-is-turning-his-paris-climate-decision-into-a-television-event/?utm_term=.d7333770af91.

[21] Chris Stirewalt, "Is Media Trump Deranged? Maybe. Dependent? For Sure," *Fox News*, May 22, 2017, http://www.foxnews.com/politics/2017/05/22/is-media-trump-deranged-maybe-dependent-for-sure. html.

[22] Brian Steinberg and Cynthia Littleton, "Cable News Wars: Inside the Unprecedented Battle for Viewers in Trump Era," *Variety*, June 13, 2017, http://variety.com/2017/tv/features/cable-news-wars-cnn-msnbc-fox-news-1202462928/.

[23] Parker, "Inside Trump's Obsession with Cable TV."

[24] Josh Marshall, "Trumpers Don't Hate Media: They Are Media Creations," *Talking Points Memo*, July 14, 2017, http://talkingpointsmemo.com/edblog/the-trumpers-dont-hate-media-they-are-media-creations.

[25] Robert Hariman, "Seeing Through Shadows," *No Caption Needed*, January 17, 2008, http://www.nocaptionneeded.com/2008/01/seeing-through-shadows/.

[26] Mahler, "CNN Had a Problem."

[27] Steinberg and Littleton, "Cable News Wars."

[28] Mahler, "CNN Had a Problem."

[29] Marche, "Celebrity Warfare."

[30] Brian Beutler, "Why the Media is Botching the Election," *New Republic*, September 13, 2016, https://newrepublic.com/article/136730/media-botching-election.

Collin Gifford Brooke

How #Trump Broke/red the Internet

Here is the testament of a man who swung a great people into his wake. Let us watch it carefully; and let us watch it, not merely to discover... what political move is to follow... [L]et us try also to... know, with greater accuracy, exactly what to guard against, if we are to forestall the concocting of similar medicine in America. – Kenneth Burke[1]

When our responses are preempted and shaped by the protocols of the network – "only 140 characters... only 'like' button option... only memes or emojis accepted" – then our critical faculties start to follow the same subroutines as the algorithm. Ping goes the phone. Jerk goes the neck. Our latent Pavlovian vulnerabilities rise to the surface, exploited by those who have entire armies of scientists – social and cognitive – at their bidding, paid handsomely to keep us monkeys holding the electronic bananas, without realizing it's a trap. – Dominic Pettman[2]

There's a story that we tell ourselves, those of us who work in education, and literacy education in particular. It's part of a long history that connects education with the (American) national interest, especially as that interest is conceived as democratic. As John Dewey explained nearly a century ago, "the realization of a form of social life in which interests are mutually interpenetrating, and where progress, or readjustment, is an important consideration, makes a democratic community more interested than other communities have cause to be in deliberate and systematic education."[3] The interdependence of democracy and education is an attitude that operates quietly and persistently in our culture, functioning in the background until it surfaces at moments of crisis. In the wake of the Second World War, rhetoric and communications scholars emphasized the importance of such training in resisting the appeals of world leaders such as Hitler. With the Russian launch of Sputnik, the United States invested heavily in their own space program as well as math and science curricula. And of course, more recently, an emphasis on technology education has been a visible cornerstone of our country's efforts to navigate a new century.

The idea that a country's welfare would rely on the quality of its education is especially true when it comes to the literacy of its citizens. We speak casually of "informed voters" who are capable of gathering information from multiple sources, evaluating that information, testing it against their own values, and selecting candidates for elected office who best represent them. This may be an ideal (or even idealistic) articulation of voter literacy, but it is one that informs curricula and media, a fundamental cultural logic upon which both our politics and our education rest.

In the aftermath of the 2016 United States Presidential Election, it should therefore serve as no surprise that a widespread call for education has been a persistent theme. Although such calls often cloak social biases, post-mortem discussions of the election frequently observed how the vote broke down along educational lines. The Pew Center reported that "a wide gap in presidential preferences emerged between those with and without a college degree."[4] Other publications were far less subtle, going so far as to label Trump voters uninformed, misinformed, ignorant, and the like. Seizing upon the question of "fake news" and the claims of so-called "filter bubbles," pundits, organizations, and even state legislatures are showing a renewed dedication to the idea of media literacy.

This chapter argues, however, that such a call is premature. We may not know for many years yet the exact combination of factors that led to Donald Trump's election. And yet, too many commentators have leapt to the conclusion that his victory was, in part or in whole, a breakdown of information and media literacy. The corresponding plan, to reinvest our educational efforts in those literacies, even where it is not motivated by resentment over the election's outcome, is almost certainly doomed to failure. If indeed the 2016 election represents a failure of American democracy, it is less an issue of voters' media literacy than it is a matter of our collective, social literacy regarding our media context.

In an essay titled "Did Media Literacy Backfire?" scholar danah boyd explains that dealing with "fake news" in all of its variations is not a simple task.[5] "It's going to require a cultural change about how we make sense of information, whom we trust, and how we understand our own role in grappling with information. Quick and easy solutions may make the controversy go away, but they won't address the underlying problems."[6] We might argue that it will require a *second* cultural change, as the first has arguably already occurred. The history of US politics is also in part a history of its delivery through communications media.[7] The 20th century bore witness to innovations such as radio, network television, cable television, and finally the early stages of the internet, and each of these was deployed to the rhetorical advantage of certain politicians.

However, a single basic logic governs them, the same logic at the heart of Dewey's insistence on democratic education. Technologies in the 20th century provided us with escalating access to political candidates; our television and computer screens were windows onto a process that provided us with increasing amounts of information. As we have moved into the 21st century, however, our modes of delivery have begun to shape not only the information we are exposed to but the processes themselves. It may sound quaint to echo Marshall McLuhan's adage that the medium is the message, but with social media, his insight has never seemed as prescient as it does today. This chapter will focus on one particular thread here, the relationship between social media and politics in the US. The full story of that relationship is still evolving, but there are specific points that might provide us with some insight into the events of 2016, and a place to begin rethinking media literacy and, by extension, its place in politics.

Social Media and the Emergence of Deliver-ative Democracy

In 2015, CNN commentator Van Jones wrote that, while Barack Obama was our country's first true internet president, we were in serious jeopardy of Donald Trump becoming the first social media president.[8] At the time, however, media pundits like Jones meant something more like the infamous joke about Trump being a comments section incarnate:

Fig. 1: Brian Gaar tweet.[9]

Unfortunately, there was more truth to this idea than people realized. While it is too early perhaps to speak definitively about the 2016 election, we can examine some of the patterns that preceded that election, trends that suggest that our "social media president" is as much about the technologies that delivered the campaign as it is about the man who currently occupies the White House. The success of Trump's campaign suggests a different model of what it meant to be an internet candidate; in certain ways, #Trump embraced the logic of the comments section rather than distancing itself from it, and this was part of the campaign's success. Commentators who expected the so-called "pivot" into some form of presidential gravitas remain disappointed, more than a year into Trump's presidency.

If Trump does indeed represent the instantiation of a comments section, then perhaps we need to turn to writers like Joseph Reagle, whose 2015 book *Reading the Comments* argues precisely against the sort of dismissal that accompanied the Twitter meme above.[10] Reagle's book is about responding to the culture of the comment section rather than ignoring it or shutting it down. In many ways, the outcome of the 2016 election functions as proof that the latter options, at least insofar as they apply to public or civic discourse, simply do not work. But even Reagle's work, tied as it is to the genre of the comment, feels quaint and ill-equipped when it comes to the largely decontextualized world of mobile-driven social media. The cultural logic of the comments section — where speed and volume often matter more than accuracy — has decoupled from those genres (news sites, weblogs, reviews) where we used to find it. Instead, it has become a zeitgeist for social media at large. A full history of that transformation would be years in the making, but we can consider briefly some of the effects that it has had on US politics.

In the early 2000s, prior to the widespread adoption of smart phones, social media was preceded by "social software," a term that danah boyd credits to Clay Shirky. At that point, following the dot-com bust of the late 1990s, the web was changing in particular ways. Static homepages were slowly giving way to weblogs, and comment sections were driving a push towards online social interaction. The collapse of commercial speculation on the web made room for a new kind of public space, one that wasn't anchored in a physical analogue. boyd explains, "Most social applications pre-boom were all about connecting people... based on a topical task even if the primary motivation to participate was random chatter."[11] At the time, online activity more closely mirrored the physical world. You visited a website the same way that you would enter a store, and participation (in the form of user reviews on products, e.g.) were understood primarily as a means of increasing interactivity and perhaps also site loyalty.

In this sense, Democratic nominee Howard Dean was perhaps the first internet candidate for president. Clay Shirky explains that the Dean campaign "put the internet to the best, most vivid, and most imaginative use it has ever gotten in any national campaign," despite their eventual failure. If nothing else, the 2004 campaign provided some important glimpses into a political process that had not changed much (technologically) for generations. Shirky suggests that the pundits failed to account sufficiently for the novelty of the internet. "Prior to MeetUp," he explains, "getting 300 people to turn out would have meant a huge and latent population of Dean supporters, but because MeetUp makes it easier to gather the faithful, it confused us into thinking that we were seeking an increase in Dean support, rather than a decrease in the hassle of organizing groups."[12]

If this phenomenon sounds familiar, it may be because *WIRED* editor Chris Anderson first introduced the idea of the long tail in the fall of 2004.[13] The ability of long-tail retailers like Netflix and Amazon to aggregate interest in niche content, without concern for geography, has been a cornerstone of our understanding of the internet for the past decade or more, and it found an early, political expression in the Dean campaign. A bricks-and-mortar retailer, concerned with overhead costs, must carefully curate the products that occupy their finite, physical spaces to meet the needs and desires of the customers who visit them. The advantages of online retail are obvious in this respect: they often have much less overhead to offset, and they can draw customers from literally anywhere in the world. When this model was blended with politics, however, as Shirky notes, the Dean campaign failed to account for those ways that voting was still a bricks-and-mortar enterprise. "Voting," Shirky offers, "is the victory of geography over affinity. Deaniacs in NYC could donate money and time... but they couldn't actually vote anywhere but NYC."[14]

In stark contrast to the overconfidence and ultimate failure of the Dean campaign, the efforts of Barack Obama's staff led to his election in 2008. As noted earlier, Obama became the United States' first internet president, a distinction that carries several layers to it. Importantly, his staff, many of whom were involved with Dean's campaign, sought both to learn lessons from 2004 and to anticipate the shifting landscape of 2008. Obama's two terms in office effectively straddled the transition from a desktop internet (focused on email and the web) to the mobile internet familiar to us today, and the campaign arguably contributed to that transition. In 2008, then-candidate Obama faced an opponent whom Bruce Bimber has described as the "last major presidential candidate in the US to run for office treating the digital media environment as distinct and separate from the larger context for political communication"[15]; while national elections cannot be reduced to single factors, there was little question that Obama's substantial digital advantage over John McCain was one of the factors in his victory.

There are many books about the role of the internet and social media in politics, making exhaustive coverage here impossible. However, we can note a few factors. Obama's campaign was the first to use web presence as something other than a mirror of offline activity. The *MyBarackObama* (MyBO) site provided campaign documents, platform statements, and the like, but it also functioned as a social hub for volunteers. The Obama campaign aggressively pursued their goals across a range of platforms; as Bimber notes, the point of this was less to find the "right" platform than it was to provide that very range to voters. "Together, the broad portfolio of communication media embraced by the campaign allowed citizens to match their own personalized interests and styles of participation to what the campaign was doing."[16] At a time when sites like Facebook were offering users new opportunities for self-expression, the Obama campaign generated tools like obamicon.me, which would convert images into the visual style and colors of the iconic Hope image designed by Shephard Fairey.

Perhaps more important than any of these specific innovations, however, was the degree to which digital tools allowed the Obama campaign to operate independently of the Democratic Party. In the week following Obama's election in 2008, David Carr wrote a column for the *New York Times* about his success, comparing the Obama campaign to Silicon Valley innovators, particularly in the ways he was able to disrupt traditional models of success. "More profoundly, while many people think that President-elect Obama is a gift to the Democratic Party," Carr writes, "he could actually hasten its demise. Political parties supply brand, ground troops, money and relationships, all things that Mr. Obama already owns."[17] Many of the distinctive features of the Obama campaign point specifically to this independence. They were able to raise more money through small donations than McCain's campaign raised in total, according to the FEC, a fact that speaks to the distribution and self-organization of Obama's volunteers. But it also points to the ways they were able to capitalize on news cycle immediacy; according to the *Huffington Post*, Obama raised $10 million through small donations during the 24 hours following the confirmation of Sarah Palin as McCain's running mate.[18] Small donations also allowed them independence; election laws don't permit individual campaigns to receive donations larger than $5,000.

According to reports from the FEC, the Obama campaign's attention to small donations persisted in 2012, as did many of their social media strategies. However, with their candidate running as an incumbent, against an opponent whose staff had ample opportunity to reflect on the successes and failures of 2008, the Obama campaign's approach was more subtle. Neither campaign was particularly aggressive digitally, although Obama's digital presence stood out for what we might think of as their "counterpunches." For example, following Clint Eastwood's speech at the Republican National Convention, where he berated an empty chair meant to signify the president, Obama tweeted a photo of himself seated in a chair at a Cabinet meeting with the brief caption, "This seat's taken." Mitt Romney and the Republican Party found themselves the object of social media counterattacks with some frequency, for comments about women, certain segments of the electorate, Romney's personal finances, and so on.

Perhaps the most significant element of Obama's 2012 campaign, however, was the degree to which digital media began to usurp the role of mass media. According to the Pew Research Center in a report on technology and politics from that year, "The changes from 2008 go beyond the candidates adding social media channels. The Obama campaign has also localized its digital messaging significantly… It has also largely eliminated a role for the mainstream press."[19] The personal data collected over the course of the 2008 campaign was converted into highly strategized micro-campaigning in 2012. A couple of months before the election, *Chicago Magazine* published a piece that asked "Can Obama data-mine his way to victory?" where they interviewed David Axelrod, Obama's chief strategist from 2008. According to Axelrod, the data analytics deployed in 2012 made their campaign from just four years prior appear "prehistoric."[20] In addition to allowing them to target crucial populations and demographics in swing states, this shift towards micro-campaigning left little room for the kinds of mass media campaigning that characterized the forty or so years prior.

This abbreviated history can only hint at the outlines of a shift that Nat Eliason has characterized as the move "from search to social," his description of the transition whose echo we can see in politics.[21] Eliason explains the transition in terms of pulling and pushing:

> You no longer enter the Internet the way you would a public library, where you browse and pick out what you want to read in peace; it's more like the Vegas strip, where you're bombarded with demands for your attention and need not exert any effort to be entertained.[22]

In terms of political campaigns, what we've seen is the slow shift away from conceiving digital campaigning as a secondary or supplemental approach. Much of this was accomplished by Obama and his staff, but the trend itself began earlier, and has perhaps come to fruition with the events of the 2016 campaign(s). If anything, though, political operatives have been slower to respond than others in our culture; we are only just now a decade removed from a presidential candidate (McCain) who felt comfortable publicly confessing his complete lack of ability with or interest in technology. Politics in the United States have shifted quickly, but it has not been entirely unprecedented.

The Election of a
"Social Media President"

There is little question that Donald Trump's campaign figured heavily on the side of what Eliason describes as the social end of the spectrum, and in that sense, describing him as our first social media president may indeed be accurate. But it is worth our time to reflect on the 2016 campaign itself, as it saw a conflict between competing models of what a "social media presidency" might entail. Considered through the lens of technology, it would be more accurate to think of the 2016 presidential race as a three-way contest, featuring the two mainstream Party candidates but including Bernie Sanders as well.

Interestingly, Sanders was the candidate whose strategies most resembled Obama's 2008 campaign, at least in terms of grassroots engagement and emergent social media activity. In an election that was ultimately contested between two candidates widely perceived to be champions of the elite (Clinton as a political elite, Trump as an economic elite), Sanders offered what his supporters claimed was an authentic alternative, more interested in social and economic justice than personal aggrandizement. Sanders' lack of technological sophistication attracted an almost ironic wave of support among younger voters, while his staff engaged those voters in ways similar to Obama in 2008. According to *Slate Magazine,*

> Online social networking has allowed Sanders supporters to reinforce one another's beliefs, so that the general shutout of Sanders by the mainstream media—and even a good deal of the leftist media—allowed Sanders to survive where he would have suffocated even in 2008. The Internet made it much, much easier for Sanders supporters to organize, with a core of young voters far more native to the Web than even Obama's base eight years ago.[23]

Speaking specifically to its organizational potential, Scott Goodstein, CEO of the company in charge of Sanders' social media, explained that "Any campaign that thinks that these are silly little things that just the kids are doing is missing how powerfully, robustly, and rapidly you can move a message or push facts around the press and rebuttals around debates."[24]

It is difficult not to hear echoes of the same entrepreneurial ethos that infused both Dean's and Obama's earlier campaign when considering Sanders. Considering how long the odds were against his nomination, and the ability of his staff to produce massive rallies and poll swings without the intervention or assistance of mainstream media, it is hard not to see Sanders' campaign as the natural outgrowth of a digital democracy begun more than a decade prior to his candidacy. Social media, for Sanders, was a means of engaging the electorate, amplifying the voices of his supporters, and personalizing his messages to them. In the words of Goodstein, Sanders' staff let "the digital team be baked into the entire DNA structure of the campaign."[25] But for its outcome, Sanders may have run the most successful social media campaign to date.

Of course, Sanders lost, and while many are still exploring (and arguing over) the reasons why, one important feature emerges. Descriptions of Obama's campaign, particularly from 2008, make note of how his team welded together personalized, grassroots media with a massively centralized command structure. If Sanders' activity represented the progressive edges of the Democratic Party, its center was emphatically occupied by the woman who became the Democratic nominee, Hillary Rodham Clinton.

In some ways, Clinton was hampered both by Obama's success and by his campaign's relative independence from the Democratic Party, which appeared to double down on Clinton's nomination from the outset in the form of super-delegates. If Sanders resembled Obama from 2008, Clinton's campaign seemed to take its cues too often from Obama 2012, but without the personalization and engagement that Obama's staff had perfected in the interim. On those few occasions where her social media activity crossed over to the mainstream, such as the infamous "Delete your account" tweet,[26] it seemed clear that the Clinton campaign was putting its energy into counterpunching, a strategy more suited to incumbents.

And yet, media coverage of the digital arm of Clinton's campaign was generally positive. That assessment, however, frequently came from looking at her activity outside of the context of media cycles. Emmy Bengtson, a former deputy social media director for Clinton, explains their team's strategy thusly: "Our strategy was fundamentally about respecting voters' intelligence: We presented the evidence of why Hillary was the superior choice for president, first over another pro-gressive and then over a lunatic."[27] There are echoes here of the assumption that Trump voters were fundamentally unintelli-gent, but setting those aside reveals a perfectly reasonable, and perhaps even desirable, model for civil, public discourse.

Furthermore, it is an ideal perfectly aligned with recent calls for renewed attention to (media) literacy. As admirable as this ideal is, hewing to this strategy was one of the primary factors that led to Clinton's defeat in the 2016 election, a conclusion that may speak more ill of social media than it does of Clinton herself or of her campaign staff. The *Huffington Post*, shortly after the election, criticized the Clinton campaign for its inattention to the "outside game," the media platforms and functions that helped candidates' messages resonate with those outside of their immediate circle of supporters.[28] It didn't help that her opponent was "outside" for nearly the entire campaign and that the contrasts between them that should have favored Clinton ultimately did not.

In many ways, Sanders and Clinton represented two competing models of digital literacy familiar to anyone who has studied that field over the past twenty years. Clinton seemed to embrace a model of digital engagement that trusted in those platforms' ability to build upon and reinforce a relatively stable understanding of literacy. As Bengtson put it, this was an approach that "respected the voters' intelligence," and, in fact, specifically catered to it.[29] Many of the early approaches to internet-based digital literacy emphasized the degree to which it could improve traditional models of literacy. Sanders' campaign resembled the intervention of social media and Web 2.0. They focused on emergent tactics, newer platforms, and strategies that had no equivalent in mass media. It was no accident that Sanders' campaign, from #FeelTheBern to SnapChat and Slack, felt fresher and more contemporary, despite a candidate in Sanders and a fairly traditional, liberal platform that might not have resonated otherwise.

It's important to distinguish the campaigns of the Democratic candidates from that of the eventual winner of the 2016 election, Republican candidate Donald Trump. All three candidates found themselves in a much different social media landscape than those that had informed previous campaigns; Sanders and Clinton offered tried-and-true strategies that had worked for earlier candidates and, in some senses, this left them ill-prepared to contest the election.

Over the next several years, we will undoubtedly learn how much of the Trump campaign strategy was intentional, and how much of it was simply a timely match between the political and media landscape with a candidate particularly well-suited to take advantage of it. To describe Trump as a "social media president" is ambiguous at best. On the one hand, his behavior on Twitter has allowed him to circumvent many of the checks that political parties and news media place on an elected official; whether or not that circumvention is strategic is difficult to say. On the other hand, commentators like Eliason—who describes the shift from search to social as "destructive"—or boyd might argue that Trump was simply in the right place at the right time, taking advantage of chaos that he has contributed to but perhaps not caused.

There is increasingly little doubt that the 2016 election was marked by interference from outside agents. Facebook officials have testified to the extent of political activity on their site that originated from outside of the United States. In one notorious example, Russian owned accounts were responsible for organized and executing pro- *and* anti-Muslim demonstrations at the same location in Houston in May of 2016. Regardless of whether or not those responsible were actively colluding with Americans, the effects of their involvement (not to mention the violence and/or property damage they aimed to provoke) had an impact on United States politics. When possible, the Trump campaign appeared to relish chaos like this, relying on the simplicity and volume of their messages that were often little more than hashtags themselves. The Trump campaign itself was a series of rallies and intemperate tweets, designed not to persuade anyone of the candidate's political platform but to aggrandize him. That such a strategy was successful owes itself to a number of different factors, of course, but there are two in particular that relate to social media.

First, Trump himself, some thirty years ago, offered the key to his media engagement in his ghost-written book *The Art of the Deal*. About the press, Trump explains:

> One thing I've learned about the press is that they're always hungry for a good story, and the more sensational the better. It's in the nature of the job, and I understand that. The point is that if you are a little different, or a little outrageous, or if you do things that are bold or controversial, the press is going to write about you... But from a pure business point of view, the benefits of being written about have far outweighed the drawbacks. It's really quite simple. If I take a full-page ad in the *New York Times* to publicize a project, it might cost $40,000, and in any case, people tend to be skeptical about advertising.[30]

The *New York Times,* in March of 2016, concluded that Trump had already received close to $2 billion in free media exposure, while barely having to spend his own money.[31] And while he was more than willing to call up morning shows and speak with them on air, Twitter functioned as an even more effective tool for this approach, one that required minimal effort and enabled him not only to dominate news cycles but to drive them.

Elsewhere in his book, Trump explains that his approach is characterized by hyperbole: "I play to people's fantasies. People may not always think big themselves, but they can still get very excited by those who do. That's why a little hyperbole never hurts."[32] For someone looking to be covered in the society pages or to garner attention for a reality television show, this is a perfectly rational and perhaps even appropriate strategy. When it comes to politics, however, Trump's behavior begins to look like intentional falsehood. In late 2016, Lauren Duca wrote about how similar Trump's tactics were to gaslighting, a form of harassment that has become all too common on social media in the past few years. As she explains, "[Trump] gained traction in the election by swearing off the lies of politicians, while constantly contradicting himself, often without bothering to conceal the conflicts within his own sound bites. He lied to us over and over again, then took all accusations of his falsehoods and spun them into evidence of bias."[33]

It is not that Trump (and his staff) are particularly adept at social media, but they were very effective in adopting a strategy that had previously been the domain of internet trolls. They engaged in hyperbole and controversy, and while the media scrambled to process and respond to their missives, they were already making other statements, whether on social media or at campaign rallies. Social media in the hands of the Trump campaign became a tool of distraction rather than edification or engagement. As Duca notes, it became a platform for "normalizing deception," with the added benefit of negating other candidates' attempts to use the platform.[34]

The Trump campaign's second approach to social media was remarkably old-fashioned, and that was the revitalization of the campaign rally. More than any other tactic perhaps, the rally was the means by which they aggregated voters across the country, particularly those in areas of the country that were not identified by the national news media as "swing states." These rallies took advantage of what rhetoricians call *affect*. Affect "describes the relative strength or weakness of bodily responses to one another and to environmental cues."[35] As a concept, affect describes the way persuasion happens physically and emotionally, and often totally unconsciously. The affective impact of gathering in crowds with thousands of other people, chanting slogans, and booing the press (and whomever else were designated villains in the moment) lent the Trump campaign a visceral appeal that had far more impact than the media suspected.

If there was a particularly effective element of the Trump campaign, it was this, their single-minded attention to the "outside game" cited earlier. The trend in US politics, from Kennedy onward, has been a steadily increased focus on the mediation of politics through our screens, first in the form of television, then our computers, and finally our phones. If nothing else, the Trump campaign managed to leverage the logic of social media (its emphasis on connection, the aggregation of geographically disparate affinity groups, et al.) in oral media. Trump's emphasis on unplanned interviews (media call-ins) and massive rallies allowed him to play to his strengths as a speaker. It is in this sense that we might describe him as our first social media president.

Breaking the Internet

If Sanders and Clinton represented the struggle between two competing models of digital literacy, Trump's victory suggests a very different lesson about the impact of social media. In particular, it raises the question about whether we can genuinely move forward. In her discussion of media literacy, danah boyd recalls the meme that spread on Facebook in the summer of 2016, a fake story about the Pope supporting Trump's candidacy.[36] While the story was obviously false, a great deal of its traction came not from people who believed it, but from Democrats themselves. She explains, "The reason so many progressives know this story is because it was spread wildly among liberal circles who were citing it as appalling and fake. From what I can gather, it seems as though liberals were far more likely to spread this story than conservatives."[37] Investigating false reports, disproving them, and publicizing their inaccuracy sounds exactly like what a media literate populace should be doing. But, in fact, the "disproof" made the story far more visible than it should have been. And as boyd explains, this is actually a conscious strategy: "Getting doubters to click on clickbait is far more profitable than getting believers because they're far more likely to spread the content in an effort to dispel the content."[38]

In other words, it's not simply a matter of locating and verifying information, when it comes to social media. The very act of sharing, even when the content is demonstrably false, serves to spread that falsehood almost as effectively. In this way, we all find ourselves delivery mechanisms for campaigns such as #Trump, and there is little evidence that we understand this problem. Improved media literacy is a noble goal, but it lags behind efforts to frustrate it and/or exploit it; in many cases, media literacy is already taken into account by those who would fool us. When Facebook launched their "real name policy" in 2012 to combat a perceived epidemic of fake accounts, for example, it had the dual effect of driving those fake accounts a little deeper into the system while disarming the potential skepticism of general users. Despite a commitment to "real" identities, Facebook itself estimates that 60 million of their accounts are fakes, but there is no incentive for them to police those accounts unless they violate terms of service. For regular users of the site who join a group, they have no reason to suspect that they are being manipulated by Russian operatives, Eastern European hackers, or the like. The group founders' profiles are likely to look much the same as their own.

Calls for improved media literacy, whether intentionally or not, place the blame for misinformation on individuals, asking them to compensate for what in the 2016 election was a series of massive failures on the parts of several institutions, including our political parties and the news media. From the asymmetry of media coverage to the violations of a number of long-held norms and customs governing political practice in this country, Lauren Duca is right to suggest that the election was an assault on democracy in this country. While Donald Trump may have been the beneficiary of that assault, he was not the source of it; the challenge posed to democracy by social media will have to be confronted on several fronts if we are to repair the damage it's caused.

Notes

1   Kenneth Burke, "The Rhetoric of Hitler's 'Battle'," *The Philosophy of Literary Form: Studies in Symbolic Action* (Berkeley, CA: University of California Press, 1973), 191–220.
2   Dominic Pettman, *Infinite Distraction: Paying Attention to Social Media* (Cambridge: Polity, 2016).
3   John Dewey, *Democracy and Education: An Introduction to the Philosophy of Education* (New York: Macmillan, 1916), 87.
4   Pew Research Center, "Behind Trump's Victory: Divisions by Race, Gender, Education," *FactTank*, November 9, 2016, http://www.pew research.org/fact-tank/2016/11/09/behind-trumps-victory-divisions-by-race-gender-education/.
5   danah boyd, "Did Media Literacy Backfire?" *Data and Society: Points*, January 5, 2017, https://points.datasociety.net/did-media-literacy-backfire-7418c084d88d.
6   boyd, "Did Media Literacy Backfire?"
7   Delivery is one of the central canons of rhetoric dating back at least two millennia. As I argue elsewhere, delivery is an important rhetorical form of identity performance. See Collin Brooke, *Lingua Fracta: Toward a Rhetoric of New Media* (Hampton, NJ: Hampton Press, 2009).
8   Van Jones, "Trump: The Social Media President?" *CNN.com*, October 26, 2015, http://www.cnn.com/2015/10/26/opinions/jones-trump-social-media/index.html.
9   Brian Gaar, Twitter post, December 7, 2015, https://twitter.com/brian gaar/status/674003276258394112. See also Andy Baio, "Tracking the

'Trump is a Comment Section Running for President' Joke," *waxy.org*, December 14, 2015, https://waxy.org/2015/12/tracking_the_trump_is_a_comment_section_running_for_president_joke/.

10 Joseph M. Reagle, Jr., *Reading the Comments: Likers, Haters, and Manipulators at the Bottom of the Web* (Cambridge, MA: MIT Press, 2015).

11 Reagle, *Reading the Comments.*

12 Clay Shirky, "Exiting Deanspace," *Extreme Democracy*, ed. Jon Lebkowsky and Mitch Ratcliffe, June 1, 2005, http://www.extreme democracy.com/chapters/Chapter15-Shirky.pdf.

13 Chris Anderson, *The Long Tail: Why the Future of Business Is Selling Less of More* (New York: Hyperion, 2006).

14 Shirky, "Exiting Deanspace," 10.

15 Bruce Bimber, "Digital Media in the Obama Campaigns of 2008 and 2012: Adaptation to the Personalized Political Communication Environment," *Journal of Information Technology & Politics* 11.2 (2014): 136.

16 Bimber, "Digital Media," 134.

17 David Carr, "How Obama Tapped Into Social Networks' Power," *New York Times*, November 9, 2008, http://www.nytimes.com/2008/11/10/business/media/10carr.html.

18 Nico Pitney, "Obama Raises $10 Million After Palin Speech," *Huffington Post*, September 4, 2008, http://www.huffingtonpost.com/2008/09/04/obama-raises-8-million-af_n_124023.html.

19 Pew Research Center, "How the Presidential Candidates Use the Web and Social Media," *Journalism & Media*, August 15, 2012, http://www.journalism.org/2012/08/15/how-presidential-candidates-use-web-and-social-media/.

20 Geoffrey Johnson, "Can Obama Data-Mine His Way to Victory?" *Chicago Magazine*, July 24, 2012, http://www.chicagomag.com/Chicago-Magazine/August-2012/Can-Obama-Data-Mine-His-Way-to-Victory/.

21 Nat Eliason, "The Destructive Switch from Search to Social," *Medium*, September 25, 2017, https://medium.com/the-mission/the-destructive-switch-from-search-to-social-250289992e30.

22 Eliason, "The Destructive Switch."

23 David Auerbach, "The Bernie Bubble," *Slate*, February 17, 2016, http://www.slate.com/articles/technology/future_tense/2016/02/the_bernie_sanders_campaign_owes_a_lot_to_social_media.html.

24 Michael Grothaus, "Inside Bernie Sanders's Social Media Machine," *Fast Company*, April 11, 2016, https://www.fastcompany.com/3058681/inside-bernie-sanders-social-media-machine.

25 Grothaus, "Inside Bernie Sanders's Social Media Machine."

26 Hillary Clinton, Twitter post, June 9, 2016, https://twitter.com/hillaryclinton/status/740973710593654784.

27 Emmy Bengtson, "I Tweeted for Hillary Clinton for a Year and a Half. I Learned Some Things," *Medium*, November 8, 2017, https://medium.

com/hillary-for-america-digital-one-year-later/i-tweeted-for-hillary-clinton-for-a-year-and-a-half-i-learned-some-things-9fb952076f25.

28 Alan Rosenblatt, "What Did Hillary Clinton Leave On The Social Media Table?" *Huffington Post*, December 2, 2016, https://www.huffington post.com/entry/what-did-hillary-clinton-leave-on-the-social-media_us_58419d99e4b04587de5de94d.

29 Bengtson, "I Tweeted for Hillary Clinton."

30 Donald J. Trump, *The Art of the Deal* (New York: Random House, 2009), 56.

31 Nicholas Confessore and Karen Yourish, "$2 Billion Worth of Free Media for Donald Trump," *New York Times*, March 15, 2016, https://www.nytimes.com/2016/03/16/upshot/measuring-donald-trumps-mammoth-advantage-in-free-media.html.

32 Trump, *Art of the Deal*, 58.

33 Lauren Duca, "Donald Trump is Gaslighting America," *Teen Vogue*, December 10, 2016, https://www.teenvogue.com/story/donald-trump-is-gaslighting-america.

34 Duca, "Donald Trump is Gaslighting America."

35 Sharon Crowley, *Toward a Civil Discourse: Rhetoric and Fundamentalism* (Pittsburgh, PA: University of Pittsburgh Press, 2006), 82.

36 boyd, "Did Media Literacy Backfire?"

37 boyd, "Did Media Literacy Backfire?"

38 boyd, "Did Media Literacy Backfire?"

Davis W. Houck

Putting His Ass in Aspirational: Golf, Donald Trump, and the Digital Ghosts of Scotland

I have nothing in common with Donald Trump.

A scion of the east coast elite, I'm a middle-class Midwesterner with neither trust funds nor black Amex cards; a grandfather with five children from three different marriages, I have no biological children but a wife who does; a loud-talking braggart whose m.o. is never to apologize, I tend toward the shy and seek to make friends first, second, and third; a seventeen-times accused sexual harasser who bragged about grabbing women "by the pussy," my mom and older sister modeled strong, accomplished, and outspoken women for me daily; when my wife and I travel we stay at the Marriott, never the Ritz-Carlton—especially not in Moscow; and, there's no need to discuss hair or skin color. Or hands. Marco was probably right.

On second thought, I suppose we do share one thing in common—an important thing—and the focus of this essay: we're both fairly accomplished golfers. I started playing golf at 12, performed well in many local tournaments held in Ohio, won something of a golf scholarship to play in college, and went on to be on the North Coast Athletic Conference All-Conference team each of my four years; and twice did I make the Division III All American team. After many years of not playing much, I picked up the game again in 2011. Today, though I don't keep an official handicap, I'm probably a +2 or +3 handicap, which means I generally shoot around par or a few under par on my home course, Killearn Country Club, in Tallahassee, Florida. I play three or four times a week with a golf-obsessed friend, Hal, usually nine holes in the evening.

Trump claims to play to a 2 or 3 handicap, owns and operates nearly 20 golf courses and resorts worldwide, stretching from Indonesia to England and Ireland and back to the US in Florida, New York, Pennsylvania, New Jersey, and California. Unsurprisingly, each of the courses and resorts is eponymously named; adjectives like "tremendous," "unbelievable," and "best" pepper the web sites and promotional literature. While he loudly and repeatedly criticized his predecessor for golfing too much, Trump is presently averaging one round of golf every 3.7 days, give or take. His favorite venue, Bedminster golf course in Bedminster, New Jersey, hosted the 2017 US Women's Open. One day he plans to be buried on said property.

On his account, golf is an "aspirational game," one reserved for the better people, which basically means white and wealthy men. Asked by *Fortune Magazine* if golf should be more accessible, Trump stated, "I think I'm in a minority, but I feel differently about golf. I feel golf should be an aspirational game, something people aspire to. People should come to golf, golf shouldn't come to them."[1] Such a view is certainly a "minority" one as golf courses continue to close around the country, but on Trump's account that outcome is just fine. After all, and in the argot of Trump, such "loser" (often public) courses closing simply means that wealthy golfers are taking their money to the more elite and private venues he favors — and owns. As golf journalist Alan Shipnuck saw first-hand, "Trump is often at his most unguarded among the people who pay for their proximity to him. Last November [2016], the President-elect hosted a cocktail reception and dinner at Bedminster on the same weekend that he was holding interviews at the club with candidates for his Cabinet. At the dinner,

Trump addressed the members of the club by saying, 'This is my real group. You are the special people. I see all of you. I recognize, like, 100% of you, just about.' Then he issued an open invitation to drop in on his Cabinet interviews the next day."[2] This was the same article in which Trump referred to the White House as a "dump." After its publication, of course, Shipnuck was called a liar in a now-common and entirely predictable early morning tweet storm by the president.

I'll return to golf in a moment. For now we need to take inventory of the past ten months of what can perhaps most generously be described as a five-alarm national dumpster fire—threatening to be six or seven. When a slaughter of more than 500 attendees at a country music festival on the Las Vegas Strip is in the news cycle for all of 48 hours, you get a sense of the ongoing national carnage and the whiplash of minute-by-minute outrage. And much of that news coverage has nothing to do with policy but with the latest puerility by a president whose administration has been openly mocked by Tennessee Republican Senator Bob Corker as "adult day care." The insults are now legion: "fake news" regardless of the outlet and truth value; "rocket man" to conduct perilous foreign policy negotiations with North Korean leader, Kim Jong-Un; "nice people on both sides" during the neo-Nazi protests in Charlottesville; the "wacky" Florida congresswoman, Fredrica Wilson, who looks "like a stripper"; the seemingly endless insults of San Juan, Puerto Rico Mayor, Carmen Yulín Cruz; the "sonofabitches" of the National Football League peacefully protesting racial inequality—the list, it seems, grows daily. All of this in the context of an investigation into Russian interference in the 2016 presidential election by Robert Mueller which threatens the legitimacy of any and all acts of the Trump administration. Whether the Special Counsel will even see the end of his own investigation remains a very real open question.

To date the administration has not passed a single piece of significant legislation—nothing on health care, tax policy, immigration, or education. Executive orders have been the order of the day since a coalition of Republicans willing and able to govern remains elusive. The ongoing civil war in the party—perhaps best represented by Breitbart's Steve Bannon and Senate Majority Leader Mitch McConnell—has recently spilled out into the open. Arizona Senator Jeff Flake is the latest Republican to denounce the Trump administration—following the rare public rebuke by former president, George W. Bush. The country's standing in the international community continues to plummet as the administration backs out of its various treaty obligations on trade, Iran, and the Paris Climate Accord. "Rocket Man" struck back with "Dotard Donny"—and the joke was on the United States.

To say that a majority of Americans are angry about the direction of the country and the person "leading" it would be to soft-pedal the current mood. The blowback has been furious and sustained—perhaps best illustrated by the many women's marches which took place on January 21, literally the first full day of the Trump administration. Estimated at well north of 2 million, and taking place in locations big and small, pussy-hatted protestors laid down the pink gauntlet before Trump could even tune in *Fox and Friends* on the White House satellite television. The resistance has only been catalyzed in the days, weeks, and months following the nation-wide protests and as speculation about Russia's influence on the election grows. Presidential approval and disapproval levels are at historic lows and highs. As I write this in late October 2017, the most recent polling indicates that "7 in 10 Americans view the Trump administration as dysfunctional."[3]

Driving the resistance to the administration is a press corps motivated in no small part by daily insult and threatened usurpation. If you're going to insist regularly on calling CNN and the *New York Times*, among many others, "fake news," frankly you're fixing for a big and protracted fight. And the fight has come to a badly prepared White House. Melissa McCa——, I mean Sean Spicer, the Ten Days of Anthony Scaramucci, and the un-Duchenne'd and perennial prevaricator, Sarah Huckabee Sanders, simply could not/cannot keep the stories straight—because the stories keep changing from

their mercurial boss. From the beginning of the Trump candidacy in a crowded Republican primary until the present day,
American journalists in particular have smelled blood in the
water. Whether it's the blood of a badly compromised former
Ukraine fixer turned campaign manager, Paul Manafort, or the
24-day tenure of National Security Advisor, Lieutenant General
Michael Flynn, the press's ferocious reporting has badly
damaged the Trump administration. The children and grandchildren of Woodward and Bernstein have inaugurated the
digital age of 24/7 political reporting with "bombshell" after
"bombshell." So many bombs have fallen and exploded at this
point that shell-shock seems to be the new normal.

Which brings us at last to our subject: the news media's
framing of the Trump presidency. With a presidency in daily
crisis, lurching from outrage to outrage, and a press trying
desperately to keep up, how does the online political media try
to communicate with its many audiences? What visual short-
hand do they employ to provide an accessible frame to help
audiences quickly understand the latest Trump story? As a
golfer, I noted that from the beginning of his candidacy certain
pictures—golfing pictures—often framed a story that had
nothing to do with golf. Furthermore, the press seemed to use
the same precious few pictures in constructing that typically
negative frame. Presented below are two of the most
ubiquitous golf frames:

Fig. 1: Trump off the tee, backside[4]

Fig. 2: Trump in the deep rough[5]

Even a non-golfer will note that these two images appear to be from the same round of golf, as the attire and golf venue seem to be identical. And in fact, the photographs were taken on July 10, 2012, at the grand opening of the Trump International Golf Links near Balmedie, Scotland.

Figure 1 shows Trump teeing off, the hole outlined by dunes and deep rough common to what is called "links golf." A links course is typically—though not exclusively in our machine age—the work of Mother Nature in which millennia of wind, sun, and rain proximate to the coast has carved out spectacular venues for golf holes. Note the absence of any trees and the presence of verdant, lush greenery. Wayward shots, I can attest first-hand, are gobbled up by the matted, thick grass; if the ball can be located, advancing it is very perilous to one's physical health let alone score. The world's very first golf course, St. Andrews, in Scotland, is a links course and serves as something of an icon and an archetype. Trump bragged that his venue near Aberdeen would be the "best course in the world" by dint of its natural beauty and the care with which the landscape was transformed into a golf course across six arduous years. In other words, Trump International Golf Links would be better than St. Andrews, to say nothing of the "rota" of other venues that annually host one of professional golf's biggest events, The British Open.[6]

Figure 2 features Trump deep in the rough and hitting a high-lofted club, perhaps a wedge. While we don't know whether Trump is attempting to pitch back to the fairway or if he's hitting a short approach to the green, suffice it to say that the "deep rough" provides a very useful framing device for any "wayward" shots. In other words, the visual understanding of the wayward, the out of bounds, the errant, and the penalized function rhetorically to provide a short-hand visual for how we are to see Trump even in a non-golfing context; golf translates fairly easily to many other contexts — especially when its penalties are visually foregrounded. Too, whether Trump has played a decent shot or not, his golf ball appears to have at least gotten airborne, which out of such thick and matter rough is often a challenge.

But beyond the golf, what can we say more generally about the golfer in each of the photographs? Having watched, participated, and in general consumed golf for the better part of 38 years, I can say unequivocally that Trump's attire is most unusual — and most unflattering. Nobody wears a white shirt on off-white trousers to play golf — especially in a links venue where occasional downpours are common. Too, when given a choice, athletes never wear white — save for the tennis players at Wimbledon who are forced to — in the age of social media (see below). While Trump's outfit in Scotland might be appropriate to paint a suburban picket fence, or leisurely spectate the local regatta, his doughy breasts threaten to be exposed by the next squall from the North Sea.

Further, and perhaps most importantly, white is NOT a slimming color. Each of the photographs allows the viewer to glimpse with some granularity the corpulence of a large man playing an aristocratic game in very luxurious confines. The effect, of course, is to dominate the frame; the sheer bulk of Trump's body draws our attention if not our critique. This is a man in nature appearing in a most unnatural way. Furthermore, the fire-engine-red hat, which would come to play a defining role in making popular Trump's Make America Great Again slogan in 2016 and beyond, is also odd. Sartorially, the baseball hat along with the white-on-white functions to render its subject as being capped, tipped, the tumescence of a fresh circumcision. For a man forever publicly obsessing over women's bleeding body parts, Trump in Scotland represents a fitting projection-in-reverse: a bloodied and bloated phallus competing against domesticated Mother Nature.

The visuals of Trump in Scotland are of course related to their conspicuous repetition and circulation. That is, as his presidency began and the gaffes, lies, failures, and general unpopularity rapidly accumulated, these images began to ricochet around the World Wide Web with dizzying speed. Daily, it seems, the images re-circulate. Why is that? Rhetorically speaking, the images function synecdochically — as short-hand frames for a president struggling mightily and rather awkwardly. As negative stories about the administration proliferate online, why not use a stock photograph that editorializes on the president?

Further, the golf frames are also especially useful to the press for the simple, but easily overlooked, reason that golf is a game played against oneself. Unlike many individual sports such as tennis, boxing, and mixed-martial-arts or track and field, golfers compete directly against only one person: the person they see in the mirror. As countless commentators have noted, Trump's many problems have usually been self-inflicted — in much the way that an errant tee-shot has only one author. Tweeting, and later deleting, "Covfefe" in the wee hours of a morning tweet storm is the functional equivalent of a snap-hook deep into the rough.[7] As such the golfing frame does a good bit of rhetorical work for commenting on a president whose self-inflicted mistakes are legion and perennial.

In addition to the link between golf and gaffes, though, even the casual observer of the photographs can easily glimpse what's not in the frame: other people. That is, each of the images captures the alone-ness of Trump; there's a solitary-ness to the pictures that captures the singularity of a persona. For a man who has made a gilded career out of self-aggrandizement, and who can turn literally any speaking event into an overdetermined referendum on his brilliance—he has "the best words" after all—the golfing photographs each carefully sequester Trump from the crowd who was following him around the links.

Before examining the stories that cluster around each of Trump's golf images, let's return to that awkward sounding term I introduced above, commonly associated with the film *Synecdoche, New York*. In his foundational 1941 essay, "The Four Master Tropes," rhetorician Kenneth Burke specifies synecdoche as a reduction, and thus a "representation."[8] That is, nouns and names often function rhetorically to stand in for a larger collective, a part for a whole, in other words. For example, to refer to an "arm" in baseball is to refer to the larger whole of a pitcher. To speak of the "White House" in political rhetoric is to refer to the executive branch of government. So, too, does the "crown" speak for a monarchy and a "ball beater" to a golfer (over)enthused by the driving range.

Russell Willerton extends our understanding of synecdoche by arguing that pictures can also abstract parts for wholes.[9] Advertising, in particular, is always on the search for provocative images that can represent a larger experience or product. Whether it's the sugar-white beaches and aquamarine waters standing in for a Sandals Resort or the emerald-colored grass representing the Ireland golfing experience, compelling images function rhetorically to link singular to whole, smaller to bigger, person to collective. Similarly, skillful political cartoonists harness the rhetorical power of synecdoche to telescope complex wholes into individual parts. Trump's hair, for example, the gossamer mane tinged with equal parts cinnamon and Clorox, now stands in for the person. As do the long red ties, the over-enunciating oval lips, and the Cheeto-hued skin. Too, the tiny presidential hands stand in, ironically, for the imperiled masculinity of the world's most powerful elected official.

Because a visual synecdoche is, by definition, a reduction and thus a representation, its rhetorical work is less to be accurate than it is to focus the attention, to draw out particulars

—in a word, to editorialize; further, that work remains to be completed by the audience, who are asked to understand a political event with visuals imported from the world of golf. As such, the rhetorical appeal of the Trump golf pictures is the ubiquity with which they might be slapped on any Trump internet story that suggests a failure, a mistake, a boner, an errant and self-induced mistake. Reduced to written text, we might say that Trump "shot himself in the foot." But, with a ready cache of visual texts to choose from, why not select the corpulent phallus in white, playing golf (poorly) deep in the weeds? By himself. Audiences also don't need to work too hard to understand the visual synecdochic work.

How best, then, to search for the two images of Trump-in-Scotland and the non-golf stories to which they get attached? If politics-as-golf is ubiquitous, where might we locate all the visuals? Until recently I didn't know that Google makes image searching/story matching rather simple. A "Trump" and "Golf" search turns up over 50 million hits. If we then click on "Images," Google retrieves countless images. Perhaps not surprisingly given our emphasis here, the very first image Google's algorithm grabs is Figure 1, Trump hitting a driver off into the distance, which accentuates his ample backside. If the Googler then right clicks on that image, eleven different options appear, including "Search Google For Image." Having selected that choice, the next screen gets us to where we want to be, namely the match between Figure 1 and the articles/ stories/tweets that use it. Scrolling down the first page of results, we see the heading, "Pages that include matching images," at which point we have our "results." And the results, Google claims, are on the order of 22,500,000! Since space (and time) does not allow me to parse so many results, I will note thematic unities as they occur in the first several pages of results; readers should get a sense for how the images function synecdochically. So yes, the astute reader can see that I'm reporting synecdochically on a synecdoche.

The very first Google hit on Figure 1 ought rightly to be singled out: Brian Beutler's *New Republic* article from

November 23, 2016.[10] Nary a word on Trump the golfer, Beutler searches at some length for the right word to describe the many outrages of Trump the person, candidate, and now president-elect. He settles eventually on "impunity," as in Trump has functioned his entire adult life without being held responsible. The corresponding image fits rather well: a singular figure striking a golf ball in the lush seaside confines; no penalties for a golf stroke are recorded. But because the image can also be read in a neutral to positive light—Trump isn't in the weeds or other hazards yet—it's not surprising that many Trump golf stories use the image. Whether the story is about Trump's upcoming Asia trip where he'll play golf with Japanese Prime Minister, Shinzo Abe, or a story that documents his many weekend trips to his golf courses, Figure 1 serves many rhetorical purposes.

Even relatively "hard" news, though, borrows the image of Trump off the Tee to frame stories about his administration. For example, a July 2017 *Newsline* article on Trump's impending G20 trip features the photograph.[11] But it also doesn't take long in parsing the Google results to read this headline: "We Know He's Huuuge, But Is He Obese?" Mark Adams at the *Men's Journal* mocks the president for his diet of "McDonald's, Burger King, KFC, and sweets."[12] As Trump's presidential ratings have continued to plummet, not surprisingly the photograph circulates heavily in political satire websites including *ClearlyRealPolitics*, where Frenjamin Branklin declares, "After Months of Trying, President Trump Qualifies for PGA Tour."[13]

No doubt some of that political satire, located in Trump off the Tee, got even more momentum with a now-famous *New Yorker* cover drawn by Barry Blitt. That April 10 illustration titled, "Broken Windows" uses the visage of Trump, featuring the high overhead finish of his driver swing, to comment critically on his destructive presidency. Blitt adds countless golf balls to show the real object of Trump's stroke(s): breaking the White House's many windows. Several things are worth noting: first, we're certain it's Trump because we've seen the swing (and the red hat) before; the destruction of the White

House (a metonym for the country) is quite purposeful, ongoing, and extensive; and that expertise in golf is being harnessed precisely to destroy the country. There's no conspiracy but a purposeful demolition—in progress. That Blitt exaggerates Trump's white-on-white corpulence is hard to miss, adding a bit of levity to the destructive tableau. Anna Swartz at mic.com put the cartoon and the photograph side-by-side in her March 31, 2017 article (Figure 3).[14] The cropped image on the left is perhaps a function of the need to navigate copyright restrictions on the image. Seeing Blitt's *New Yorker* cover and the wide circulation it received changes how we see the image on the right. We might plausibly guess that, following the April release of the magazine, the photograph (re)circulated in contexts far less amenable to the Trump presidency. Not surprisingly, and while I don't have the space to detail the extent to which political cartoonists borrow the image, Blitt is not alone when it comes to re-drawing the landscape, not the golfer, to comment rather directly on the Trump administration.

Fig. 3: Two Trumps.[15]

Turning to Figure 2, we should say a few more words about Trump in the deep rough before examining how it functions rhetorically as a news frame. Unlike Figure 1, Trump the golfer is dominated in this photograph by the deep rough and its conspicuous mounding; he appears to be in something resembling a grassy hollow. Here we can borrow again from Kenneth Burke. Burke is best known for his dramatistic pentad—a methodological tool that suggests five possible focuses for discovering what is important when studying a narrative or text or picture. The five are agent, act, purpose, scene, and agency (similar to the who, what, when, where, and how from journalism). In Figure 1 the agent is ascendant; visually the golfer is, if not in charge of his environs, at least driving them, quite literally.[16] However, presumably later in the round, the scene now dominates the red-hatted agent who hacks away at the threatening landscape. The composition of the photograph is such that the foregrounded blades of grass appear almost as big as the golfer—who bulked rather large in Figure 1. Now that same golfer appears to be in the process of being nearly swallowed up by the terrain; only a taut rictus and a well struck (?) shot played with a high-lofted club can redeem the perilous situation. The optics, in other words, are most inauspicious for a would-be president fighting hard to get back in play.

Not surprisingly, many stories that use the Trump in the deep rough photograph feature the more colloquial "weeds" in story headlines. A CNBC story, for example, is headlined, "Trump's $550 Million Golf Empire May Be in the Weeds."[17] A second and very predictable and prominent use for the photograph stems from Trump's near-constant criticism of President Obama during the 2016 campaign for playing too much golf. Not only does this frame directly reference golf, but it does double duty as a critique of Trump's blatant hypocrisy for exceeding his predecessor in trips to the links. In a CNN "Inside Politics" video story, for instance, the photograph is used to frame a story that argues, in part, "This weekend marks Pres. Trump's 8th week visiting a Trump property, but on the trail he said as President he'd never want to leave the White House."[18] Two weeks later, CNN again used the photograph in a story by Kevin Liptak, the headline of which reads, "Trump, Who Scorned Obama's Golf Habits, Outpacing Him in Rounds."[19]

By August, and with devastating testimony of fired former FBI Director James Comey, Special Counsel Robert Mueller's ongoing investigation into Russian interference and possible collusion with Trump officials, the endless iterations of his failed efforts to repeal the Affordable Care Act, and his dismal poll numbers, Trump in the deep rough was more apt than ever. To make matters worse, later that month the Secret Service reported that it would soon be out of money to protect the president; he and his family's near constant (golf) travel, including racking up more than $60,000 in golf cart rental fees just at Mar-a-Lago and Bedminster, (re)ignited use of the photograph.[20] And because there's literally a tweet for everything, the story included one from Trump in 2014: "We pay for Obama's travel so he can fundraise millions so Democrats can run on lies. Then we pay for his golf."

And while the Trump in the deep rough frame has never not been in fairly constant circulation, it spiked again in mid-September with an early morning barrage of re-tweets, one involving an edited video sequence of the president hitting a shot off the tee and the ball striking Hillary Clinton in the back as she boards an airplane and collapses. British writers at the *International Business Times* seized on the photograph to frame its story, headlined "'You're a Child': Twitter Reacts as Trump Shares Clip of Him Hitting Clinton with a Golf Ball."[21] Apparently, the fifteen-times-accused sexual harasser couldn't quite help himself on a Sunday morning, despite increasing tensions with a nuclear North Korea. The badly edited video was quite literally the shot heard-round-the-world—at least for a news cycle, which in Trumplandia means about an hour.

As I briefly alluded to above, Trump's choice of white attire to play golf in Scotland was bad at multiple levels, not the least of which is, in our Age of Photoshop, what can be done with light-colored clothing. That is, as Figure 4 reveals, the internet has had no small fun at Trump's expense with this photograph:

Fig. 4: Fecal Trump.[22]

The image of a soiled Trump-in-Scotland remains a staple among Trump haters—which means it circulates a lot. The doctored photograph frequently appears on Twitter and other social media platforms, typically with stories about Trump being a "leaker." Very infrequently does the image appear in "mainstream" media, but back in June 2017, and on the heels of the "covfefe" kerfuffle, MSNBC's *Morning Joe* host, Joe Scarborough, put the anal in analogy: "'Well yes. It would be like somebody pooping their pants and then people looking at it and saying 'oh that's modern art don't you understand,' Scarborough said as the rest of the panel laughed."[23]

The frame of a stumbling, lurching Trump being comforted by a playing companion for having shat himself forms a significant part of the vernacular web, where photoshopped images proliferate to perform the work of comedy, putdown, and invective. The image is perhaps best contextualized as the 21st century's version of the Hans Christian Andersen tale, "The Emperor's New Clothes." While material "statues" of a naked and bloated Trump continue to appear in public venues, Fecal Trump is the cruder digital version of the 19th-century original. Instead of no clothes, the image of soiled golf pants functions rhetorically to undermine any and all claims to the legitimacy of a Trump presidency. There are many expressions to convey the sentiment that someone has, perhaps unknowingly, incriminated themselves: "hoisted by his own petard"; "stepping in it"; "showing his ass," etc. As in Figure 1, Trump is showing his corpulent ass—and his bad choice of golf slacks has revealed it for the whole world to see. Or at least the World of the Wide Web.

Coda

As November dawns, the Trump presidency is in grave peril: his approval numbers continue to tank; the Mueller investigation has issued its first salvo of indictments; key players continue to flee the administration; GOP elected officials have begun condemning his puerile behavior; world leaders try to hide their embarrassment; the alt-right of neo-Nazis and the Klan continue to speak loudly in support of him; significant legislation remains elusive; the federal courts steadily litigate and overrule his executive orders; and the "fake news" he so frequently derides turns out to be rather accurate even as he's unwittingly emboldened a new generation of investigative journalism.

Whether Trump is impeached, forced to resign or even, god forbid, serves out his term, golf will remain a constant; it appears to be his one extended psychic reprieve in the face of an onslaught he never saw coming. His golf acuity allows him still to brag, with a semblance of reality, about his abilities. No doubt we will see a tweet in the foreseeable future about shooting his age.[24] As the winter approaches he'll likely flee further south to Mar-a-Lago and the Trump properties around Palm Beach County. And because golf will remain a constant for a presidency in which political chaos bordering on anarchy reigns, the red tipped, white-on-white digital ghosts of Scotland will remain a ready frame in our "unhinged" moment.

Notes

1   Daniel Roberts, "Donald Trump: Let Golf Be for the Rich Elite," *Fortune Magazine*, July 1, 2015, http://fortune.com/2015/07/01/donald-trump-golf-rich-elite/.

2   Alan Shipnuck, "First Golfer: Donald Trump's Relationship With Golf Has Never Been More Complicated," *Golf Magazine*, August 1, 2017, http://www.golf.com/tour-news/2017/08/01/president-donald-trump-relationship-golf-more-complicated-now.

3   John Wagner and Scott Clement, "'It's Just Messed Up': Most Think Political Divisions as Bad as Vietnam Era, New Poll Shows," *Washington Post*, October 28, 2017, https://www.washingtonpost.com/graphics/2017/national/democracy-poll/?hpid=hp_hp-top-table-main_democracy-poll-830am-1-winner%3Ahomepage%2Fstory&utm_term=.f95d86ebdb25.

4   Image featured in Shipnuck, "First Golfer."

5   Image featured in Rafael Bernal, "Golf Tournament Moving from Trump Course to Mexico," *The Hill*, June 1, 2016, http://thehill.com/latino/281877-trump-golf-course-losing-major-event-to-mexico.

6   The "rota" or rotation of courses hosting the Open Championship is determined by the Royal and Ancient Golf Club of St. Andrews (R&A); it presently includes 9 different golf courses.

7   The dreaded "snap hook" is a rather low and violent right-to-left careening shot that no golfer sees coming. Even professionals hit an occasional "snapper" that usually is quite penal. The effect is deeply disconcerting, too, because the shot at impact often feels very solid.

8   Kenneth Burke, "Four Master Tropes," *The Kenyon Review* 3 (1941): 421–38.

9   Russell Willerton, "Visual Metonymy and Synecdoche: Rhetoric for Stage-Setting Images," *Journal of Technical Writing and Communication* 35 (2005): 3–31.

10 Brian Beutler, "This Single Concept Explains Trump's Many Outrages," *New Republic*, November 23, 2016, https://newrepublic.com/article/138975/single-concept-explains-trumps-many-outrages.

11 RT, "May, Trump to meet privately at G20 Summit," July 6, 2017, https://newsline.com/may-trump-to-meet-privately-at-g20-summit/.

12 Mark Adams, "We Know He's Huuuge, But Is He Obese?" *Men's Journal*, n.d., http://www.mensjournal.com/health-fitness/articles/is-donald-trump-obese-an-investigation-w462910.

13 Frenjamin Branklin, "After Months of Trying, President Trump Qualifies for PGA Tour," *Clearly Real Politics*, June 30, 2017, https://www.clearlyrealpolitics.com/donald-trump-professional-golfer/.

14 Anna Swartz, "'The New Yorker' Takes Aim at Trump Again with Latest Cover," *MIC.com*, March 31, 2017, https://mic.com/articles/172797/the-new-yorker-takes-aim-at-trump-again-with-latest-cover#.EifP7eBXD.

15 Image featured in Swartz, "'The New Yorker' Takes Aim."
16 Kenneth Burke, *A Grammar of Motives* (Berkeley, CA: University of California Press, 1969). Pentadic analysis is designed, in part, to determine which key term dominates (act, agent, agency, scene, and purpose), thus imparting philosophic and motivational importance into how an event is understood by a given person.
17 Tim Mullaney, "Trump's $550 Million Golf Empire May Be in the Weeds," *CNBC*, July 23, 2015, https://www.cnbc.com/2015/07/23/trumps-550m-golf-empire-may-be-in-the-weeds-experts.html.
18 "Trump's 13th Golf Course Visit in 65 Days," *CNN.com*, March 27, 2017, http://www.cnn.com/videos/tv/2017/03/27/ip-e-block-trump-golfing.cnn.
19 Kevin Liptak, "Trump, Who Scorned Obama's Golf Habits, Outpacing Him in Rounds," *CNN.com*, April 10, 2017, http://www.cnn.com/2017/04/09/politics/trump-outpacing-obama-golf/index.html.
20 Jacob Weindling, "Donald Trump is Rapidly Depleting the Secret Service's Budget," August 21, 2017, accessed at https://www.pastemagazine.com/articles/2017/08/donald-trump-is-rapidly-depleting-the-secret-servi.html.
21 Jason Murdock, "'You're a Child': Twitter Reacts as Trump Shares Clip of Him Hitting Clinton with a Golf Ball," *International Business Times*, September 17, 2017, http://www.ibtimes.co.uk/youre-child-twitter-reacts-trump-shares-clip-him-hitting-clinton-golf-ball-1639690.
22 Image featured in "Did Trump Really Have Diarrhea During Golf Game?" *ThatsFake.com*, April 11, 2017, http://www.thatsfake.com/trump-really-diarrhea-golf-game/.
23 NA, "Trump is Like a Kid Pooping his Pants," *Nova Magazine*, June 18, 2017, https://www.nova-magazine.net/donald-trump-is-like-a-kid-pooping-his-pants/.
24 Shooting one's age refers to, in Trump's case, shooting a 71 (his age) or lower during a round of 18 holes. Among golfing aficionados, it's not quite the holy grail, but it's a very consequential achievement.

Joshua Gunn

Donald Trump's
Perverse Political Rhetoric

Unquestionably by the time this chapter appears in print, US President Donald J. Trump will have said something more obnoxious than when I originally composed it. As I write, Trump is publicly sparring with the widow of a slain soldier over what he said during a condolence call to her,[1] and before this, oodles of outrageous ejaculations,[2] perhaps most famously his private admission to an entertainment reporter that his celebrity permitted him to sexually assault women.[3] The punditry's preoccupation with Trump's vulgar ventilations started long before he was the Republican presidential nominee. He was widely critiqued for bragging he could "shoot somebody" openly on 5th Avenue and not "lose any voters,"[4] and later for ventriloquizing a woman at a New Hampshire rally who declared that Ted Cruz was a "pussy," leading Annie Lowrey of *New York Magazine* to suggest that the slur is emblematic of "Trump's magnetism and psychosis."[5] Along similar lines, Trump's xenophobia has led many to suggest he is a fascist or at least "borrows from the fascist playbook,"[6] bringing to mind Pink Floyd's bestselling meditation on psychosis and fascism, *The Wall* ("Mother should I build the wall? / Mother should I run for president?"). He's been widely dismissed as a demagogue too,[7] and largely because the success of his populist appeals appears to transcend reason—not to mention dumbfound political scientists overly wed to a "rational choice" model that has no place for culture or feelings.[8]

A common tendency of journalists, pundits, cultural critics, and anyone who follows politics is to distinguish Trump's person from his public persona by suggesting a dismissive label for the latter and suggesting the former has simply got to be more reasonable (references to *The Wizard of Oz* were frequent during the last US presidential election). Of course, in the era of reality television it is routine to confuse "real life" with "screened life" because that is the presumed illusion of the genre.[9] And, of course, it goes without saying that the contemporary politician strives to encourage a similar, cynical perception, which is perhaps why a number of mental-health experts are willing to violate professional propriety to diagnose Trump as a textbook example of "narcissistic personality disorder," characterized by grandiosity, exaggerated self-importance, and a lack of empathy.[10]

Although the narcissism of Trump's public remarks is undeniable, the trouble with labeling his person a narcissist — or a psychotic, fascist, or demagogue — is that it is perceived as a dismissive gesture that ignores Trump's *rhetoric*, thereby eliding the perhaps all-too-conveniently cynical distinction between "the show" and "the real person" upon which Trump relies so heavily. Indeed, what's characteristically different about Trump's political discourse is that he *resists* the conflation of his rhetoric with his person, and that he persistently avoids taking responsibility for his *words*. Besides, few of Trump's supporters would admit to voting for a hateful, psychotic person. Rather, many of his supporters seem to believe that "Trump knows it's all a joke," that his extremist, sexist, and racist remarks are part of a middle-finger prank that they are "in" on, and that almost everything Trump says is delivered with a wink. In other words, many voters do not so much identify with the literal meaning of his obnoxious pronouncements — although the emboldened public spectacles of self-styled Nazis in recent months is a notable exception[11] — but rather with the feelings of anger, frustration, and... mirth.

To be sure, Trump's rhetoric seduces or "hystericizes" audiences,[12] however, most scholars have thankfully stopped assuming that it is taken seriously only by the tone deaf. Trump's appeal is humorous, ironic, and double-voiced, and however odious his presumed views, many Trump voters harbor at least a tacit belief that the man behind the curtain is more decent and upstanding than his morally abhorrent stumping would seem to suggest. We are supposed to believe these days that campaigning is a put-on, a crafted, artful deception, which is the tactic that made P.T. Barnum rich with the Fiji Mermaid.[13] While it is not as pronounced in his presidential rhetoric as it was during the campaign, artful deception is Trump's modus operandi: after learning you've been conned, you keep your silence "in good fun" so that you can enjoy watching others get duped, or rather, so that you can watch the "political establishment" go nuts.[14] Trump knows Obama and Ted Cruz are US citizens, and yet... He knows global warming was not created to protect Chinese commercial interests, and yet... Artful deception is certainly reflected in Trump's key rhetorical device, *paralipsis*, which my friend and colleague Jennifer Mercieca brilliantly introduces to explain how Trump is permitted to say "things other candidates can't."[15]

Because artful deception is central to Trump's rhetoric, I think it is misleading to describe the president as a demagogue, fascist, or psycho if only because such labels fail to capture the skillful way in which Trump's rhetoric affirms and denies at the same time, cleaving his behavior from his presumed personhood, and this during a time in which the art of politics encourages their convergence, conflation, or confusion. It is the cynical suspicion of the difference between what Trump says and who he "really" is — the smirking, presumed difference — that has "changed politics" and confounded pundits in recent years.[16]

Fascism and psychosis are marked by an inability to understand or accept consensus reality, an inability to recognize limitation and the meaning of the word "no," an inability or disregard for what most folks consider to be the normative, common sense world. Fascists and psychotics do not live in our world, nor do they understand why what they say or do is wrong. Donald Trump seems to know that the offensive things he says and does are offensive, but he says and does them anyway. Trump knew his suggestion that Mitt Romney would have provided oral sex for his endorsement in 2012 was outrageous, but he said it anyway.[17] Trump knew bragging about the size of his penis during a Republican primary debate was juvenile, but he did it anyway.[18] Given the often-sadistic (and sexual) character of Trump's rhetoric, it is more typical of *perversion*, a rhetoric typified by a deliberate and knowing deviation from assumed "norms." Trump's speech is best understood a textbook example of perverse rhetoric.

Three Senses of Perversion: Common, Freudian, & Lacanian

In the common use of the term, "perversion" is usually understood as a departure from normalcy broadly conceived, and certainly Trump's campaign can be said to have perverted the assumed norms of electoral politics. In this first sense, then, Trump's rhetoric is patently perverse because the rhetor does not "play by the rules," and in so doing, has introduced the public to what is arguably the first, large-scale instance of what I'm calling *political perversion* in our time. Sure, we witnessed a form of political perversion with Richard Nixon's campaigns and presidency, and there is a sense in which all political innovations, such as Barack Obama's once novel use of social media for campaigning, are "perverse." But Trump's vulgar voice and grandiloquent gaffs mark his rhetoric as the most conspicuously, politically perverse.

Among scholars and clinicians perversion has a second, more psychoanalytic sense. Owing to the profound influence of Sigmund Freud, perversion is usually understood as a sexual aberration from *an assumed* normalcy—the proverbial peeping tom peering into the window of an undressing person, or the attribution of sexual power to a high-heeled shoe (a "fetish"). Until Freud's intervention, perversion was wrongly equated with homosexuality; however, this view has not held sway for decades. Insofar as humans have sexual pursuits *beyond* biological reproduction, all of us are to greater or lesser degrees "perverse." In the clinic, perversion has been replaced by the term "paraphilia," and, in the law courts, typically only considered criminal in the absence of mutually informed consent.

Yet among a smaller subset of academics who work with the theories of Jacques Lacan, perversion can be understood in a third sense: perversion is a kind of *structure* that inheres in culture *through* people. This is to say, perversion is a strategy that one adopts early in one's life to relate to others (the more common strategy is neurosis, and most of us adopt neurosis). One adopts such a structure by internalizing a series of relationships toward others (sort of like how one repeatedly makes connections with other people in parenting, friendships, partnerships, and so on). For the rest of this section I try to unpack the perverse structure so that readers can more easily follow how I arrive at my conclusions about Trump's rhetoric. I warn, however, it is a bit technical and that readers more interested in my analysis can skip to the next section.[19]

According to psychoanalyst Jacques Lacan, people are oriented toward others predominately as neurotics, psychotics, or perverts. Most of us are neurotic, less of us are psychotic, and even less of us are perverse in our dispositions. These dispositions form early in life, mostly in relation to our parents as our first or primary "others," and interactions with these first others help to craft the template for how we tend to interact with the social world as grown-ups. Learning how to relate to others is akin to learning to ride a bicycle, and once one adopts a particular way of riding or relating she tends to stick with it, eventually automatically or compulsively without thinking about it.

The classical neurotic comes into the world with a primary bond or identification with one parent (usually the mother), but when confronted with a second parent (historically a father) we are made to give up that primary bond through a kind of sharing (which is, of course, the point of pre-school and kindergarten: "SHARE!" is the demand, but it's experienced as

"NO!"). As young people, we learn that we can substitute the original (maternal) bond with other bonds, initially with "transitional objects" — such as a stuffed animal or blanket — but eventually with other people such as the second parent, an aunt or uncle, the family dog or cat, siblings, friends, and so on, all of whom reference the social world broadly construed. The establishment of a neurotic structure, then, entails two moves: first, an alienation from the primary parent with the introduction of a second parent who demands that we share ("You cannot have mommy all to yourself!"); and second, a separation from the primary parent as an individual with the power to speak ("I am Josh Gunn; I am not my mother"). This dance inculcates the neurotic into culture because the second parent comes to represent society, replete with rules on how to behave, what is inappropriate, what to feel guilty about, and so on. Basically, as young persons, when we are confronted with the fact that there are more folks to love than the primary parent, we become social creatures. Empirically, most of us are neurotics, psychologically alienated and separated from our parents; we fumble about in life forging various transformed bonds with parents and substitute bonds with friends and loved ones.

The psychotic never learns how to give up or create substitute bonds, nor that these are even possible, so there is neither alienation nor separation. The person with a psychotic disposition never severs itself from the primary relation, and thus dwells anon, as Fred Schneider sings, in their "own private Idaho." The person with a psychotic structure may function very well in society, but s/he lives in their own world without ever truly engaging with others as others; the psychotic moves through the world with an awkward play of "match up," and any stark incongruity is experienced by the rest of us who see it as a "psychotic break." Sometimes such breaks are violent, but strictly speaking a psychotic does not function in a normative, moral universe.

The rare, perverse disposition entails a weird middle-way between the neurotic and the psychotic: s/he knows at some level a second parent denies an exclusive bond with the primary parent ("No!"), but s/he denies or "disavows" the denial. Put in Oedipal terms, the pervert hears the dad's "no," knows that there is supposed to be a break with mom, but refuses to give her up nonetheless: there is alienation from the primary parent because the child knows there are others in the world, but he or she denies it and, consequently, there is no separation from the primary bond. The pervert refuses or *disavows* the social logic of substitution, even if s/he knows how to (pretend to) do it.

The unusual adult person who exhibits the perverse structure relates to others in alternately cruel and seductive ways—in ways that may seem to "connect" but, in reality, do not: the pervert refuses to accept the rules that everyone follows as legitimate, and follows them only insofar as it is a "game" to get what s/he wants. Instead, the pervert may play along for a while, but eventually metes their own rules on others, even fashioning themselves as an "instrument" or "tool" of some grander purpose. The pervert issues different rules as a kind of defense or shield from accepting the rules everyone else follows.

From the outside, especially from the neurotic perspective, the pervert seems to enjoy his or her transgressions, or appears to take great pleasure in manipulating, exploiting, or punishing others (such as with sadism); non-perverts might even regard the pervert with jealousy and awe. The pervert stands before us in a trench coat and, FLASH, we are made to witness their nakedness; we assume they are taking great pleasure in our shock. But, at least according to Lacan, this is not so. Strangely, the pervert's transgressions are defenses and not in pursuit of pleasure, but rather constitute various iterations of the disavowal. Because the pervert is beholden, in a sense, to the primary parental bond he or she is in a position of unbearable passivity; the transgressions and impositions of his or her own symbolic regime are an attempt to assume an active role, to get some certainty, to create a sense of stability through control. Pleasure is usually regarded as a loss of control; that is not what the pervert is after. Inviting the gaze of others and controlling it are paramount.

The perverse structure can admittedly get confusing, and this is precisely because the pervert is lodged in a fundamental ambivalence between two Others, so to speak. The key is to recognize that there are two figures in the pervert's (infantile) scenario: the original Other (mother) who has unbridled access to him or her, and the second Other (father or parent) whom the pervert disavows. The pervert believes that s/he makes the first Other whole and complete (hooray!), but this is ultimately a passive position (boo!); the pervert thus attempts to achieve an active position through a parade of disavowals, both recognizing and denying social order simultaneously. The adult pervert is aware of social norms but denies them, or abides them only insofar as they can be played to their advantage in service of some grand Other that only he or she alone can perfect (de facto the original bond, but later God, the nation state, "the American people," and so on). This is why the pervert often registers the tones of prophecy, declaring a path to security and new world order by punishing an "alien" who threatens the way things used to be ("We'll build a wall!").

Stumping Perversion

While many would consider it inappropriate to diagnose Trump as a *clinical* pervert, it seems to me there is no question that his rhetoric evinces a perverse structure. This is, at least, a partial explanation for why Trump is said to get away with statements and gaffs that would disqualify any other candidate today: he simultaneously denies the reality he asserts. As the hallmark of perversion, disavowal registers at almost every level of Trump's discourse. At the level of the statement, Trump decries journalist Megyn Kelly as a "bimbo" but later "pleads ignorance."[20] At the level of style, Trump's comb-over and ill-fitting suits are much derided but he persists on sticking with the look. At the level of genre—such as at a press conference or a news program interview—he repeatedly violates expectations but proclaims victory at following the form "beautifully." Because of length constraints I draw the reader's attention to one operatic and conspicuous example of Trump's politically perverse rhetoric: Trump's "press conference" with the alleged victims of Bill and Hillary Clinton's sexual improprieties.

Fig. 1: Trump holds a press conference with women who accused Bill Clinton of sexual assault, and one who claimed inappropriate legal tactics by Hillary Clinton. From left to right: Kathleen Wiley, Juanita Broaddrick, Donald J. Trump, Kathy Shelton, and Paula Jones. Photo Evan Vucci/Associated Press.[21]

Immediately prior to the second presidential debate with Hillary Clinton in early October 2016, Trump conducted a surprise press conference with three women who claimed to have been sexually assaulted by President Bill Clinton, and a fourth woman whose rapist was defended by Hillary Clinton. The conference was offered in the wake of the controversy ignited by the leak of a tape in which Trump bragged to an *Access Hollywood* reporter that he was able to sexually assault women because of his celebrity. Such a spectacle is a structured perversion, the disavowal of a presumed moral order at the same moment of its re-inscription: superficially the claim of the spectacle here is that the Clintons are guilty of legal and moral crimes while Trump's "locker room talk" was merely talk.

But consider this affective or feeling-based "press confer-ence" inspired by Roger Stone and orchestrated by Charles Johnson, Steve Bannon, and Jared Kushner less directly:[22] with this media spectacle sexual assault is *not* critiqued as much as it is underscored as a *norm*. This is to say, Trump's braggadocio with Clinton "victims" is in keeping with the actual order of things, where women are trafficked as objects of communica-tion between men. Trump is just doing what is actually in the underlying order of things, disavowing that he has done anything wrong by exposing the obscenity that underwrites political power. Here, too, is the "both-sides" logic of moral equivalency we hear a year later in Trump's abhorrent press conference on Charlottesville violence, that antifa protesters are just as responsible for racist violence as the white suprema-cists,[23] as if to say, "I'm not responsible because he did it too." The power of prophecy is precisely its rootedness in feelings of infantile omnipotence.

There is No Man Behind the Curtain, Or, Trump is a Curtain

Such feelings of omnipotence are worrisome in a national figure, especially because a small, belligerent state surrounded by China has a hydrogen bomb, which threatens to end this episode of reality television in mutually assured destruction. And speaking of endings, I should come to one. In this chapter I am arguing that Trump's rhetoric is representative of a perverse structure endemic to US culture and which finds expression—indeed, it has always been there—in spectacle politics. I will go one step further, where many scholars are probably are unwilling to go: Trump *is* a pervert. Were he a psychotic or fascist, the double character of his rhetorical appeals would not be in play, nor would he continue to main-tain the belief among his followers that he is really a decent guy behind an angry mask, punking the political establishment: *Trump is the political establishment in more ways than one, pointing up the obscenity that has always been there, just not broadcast so conspicuously.* The Trump persona suggests a perverse structure because Trump appears to admit at times that his racist, sexist, and xenophobic rhetoric is offensive to many, but he delivers it anyway, certain that he is giving "the true public" — the increasingly un-silent majority — what it wants. Just look at the size of that inaugural crowd!

As most medical professionals and professional critics would likely agree, it is usually a mistake to confuse a politician's rhetoric or persona with his or her person, for doing so often leads to disappointment, and sometimes the election of demagogues and fascists to office. From a scholarly perspective, however, I tend to agree with those who argue that our persons are not essences, neither reducible to biology or psychology or the language we borrow, and that we are all in some sense scripted (e.g. "posthumanism").[24] The self represents an accrual of words and deeds and human relations discernable only by interacting with others. In this qualified sense, to say that Trump is a pervert is to assert that Trump is his rhetoric. So are we all.

But one need not go that far with me and my posthumanist comrades — at least in theory. We have pragmatic, political concerns too, and at our present conjuncture perhaps these concerns could benefit from some strategic essentialism to save lives: insofar as Trump's perverse strategy is to keep his followers in constant doubt about his sincerity, perhaps the only way to resist his sadism is to deliberately make the mistake of conflating personae with personhood in ostentatious ways. By scholarly habit, my tribe has been trained to say that Trump's rhetoric is perverse, or evinces a perverse structure, not that "Trump is a pervert." But perhaps that training, which is unquestionably a play-by-the-rules neurosis particular to the academy, is a handicap in today's larger, political conversation? Perhaps we should insist that Trump is nothing more than his persona, that the persona and his person are one and the same, that Trump on the stump is all there is — that *there is nothing more to Trump than his spectacle*. As co-creators of popular perception, this spectacle includes us, too.

Author's Note: For a more in-depth and academic explanation of the arguments sketched in this chapter, see my "On Political Perversion," *Rhetoric Society Quarterly* 48 (2018): forthcoming.

Notes

1 Mark Landler and Yamiche Alcindor, "Trump's Condolence Call to Soldier's Widow Ignites Imbroglio," *New York Times*, October 18, 2017, https://www.nytimes.com/2017/10/18/us/politics/trump-widow-johnson-call.html.

2 For a convenient if not repulsive list, see "Yes, The President of the United States Really Has Said This," *Marie Claire*, July 19, 2017, http://www.marieclaire.co.uk/entertainment/people/donald-trump-quotes-57213.

3 "Transcript: Donald Trump's Taped Comments About Women," *New York Times*, October 8, 2016, https://www.nytimes.com/2016/10/08/us/donald-trump-tape-transcript.html.

4 Katie Reilly, "Donald Trump Says He 'Could Shoot Somebody' and Not Lose Voters," *Time*, January 23 2016, http://time.com/4191598/donald-trump-says-he-could-shoot-somebody-and-not-lose-voters/.

5 Annie Lowrey, "Hearing Donald Trump Refer to Ted Cruz as a 'Pussy' Told Me Everything I Need to Know About His Campaign," *New York Magazine*, February 8, 2016, http://nymag.com/daily/intelligencer/2016/02/trump-sums-up-candidacy-with-vulgar-cruz-slam.html.

6 Gianni Riotta, "I Know Fascists; Donald Trump is No Fascist," *The Atlantic*, January 16, 2016, https://www.theatlantic.com/international/archive/2016/01/donald-trump-fascist/424449.

7 Greg Sargent, "Donald Trump Is A Highly Skilled Demagogue," *The Washington Post*, January 26, 2016, https://www.washingtonpost.com/blogs/plum-line/wp/2016/01/26/donald-trump-is-a-highly-skilled-demagogue-this-one-chart-proves-it/?utm_term=.b3614141e3a1.

8 "Rational Choice Theory" (RCT) or simply "choice theory" is a model for understanding social and/or economic behavior in terms of reflective, goal-oriented thinking that is self-interested. That is, RCT suggests people make the most rational choice to achieve their own goals. In the United States, the framework dominated research in political science until relatively recently. For a critique, see Hélène Landemore, "Politics and the Economist-King: Rational Choice Theory and the Science of Choice?" *Journal of Moral Philosophy* 1 (2004): 177–96.

9 Bustie, "I Was on Reality TV: Behind the Scenes Secrets of Faking Real Life," *Huffington Post*, May 1, 2014, https://www.huffingtonpost.com/bustle/i-was-on-reality-tv-faking-real-life_b_4823714.html.

10 Henry Alford, "Is Donald Trump Actually a Narcissist? Therapists Weight In!" *Vanity Fair*, November 11, 2015, https://www.vanityfair.com/news/2015/11/donald-trump-narcissism-therapists. Also see Bandy Lee, ed., *The Dangerous Case of Donald Trump* (New York: St.

Martin's Press, 2017).

11   Rosie Gray, "Trump Defends White-Nationalist Protesters: 'Some Very Fine People on Both Sides'," *The Atlantic*, August 15, 2017, https://www.theatlantic.com/politics/archive/2017/08/trump-defends-white-nationalist-protesters-some-very-fine-people-on-both-sides/537012/.

12   For an academic elaboration of the hysterical element of political discourse, see Joshua Gunn, "Hystericizing Huey: Emotional Appeals, Desire, and the Psychodynamics of Demagoguery," *Western Journal of Communication* 71 (2007): 1–27.

13   "The Feejee Mermaid," *Hoaxes.org*, n.d., http://hoaxes.org/archive/permalink/the_feejee_mermaid. For a lucid and amusing account of artful deception as a popular discourse, see James W. Cook, *The Arts of Deception: Playing with Fraud in the Age of Barnum* (Cambridge, MA: Harvard University Press, 2001).

14   The opinion columns of conservative commentator David Brooks are good examples; see "No, Not Trump, Not Ever," *New York Times*, March 18, 2016, https://www.nytimes.com/2016/03/18/opinion/no-not-trump-not-ever.html?_r=0.

15   Jennifer Mercieca, "How Donald Trump Gets Away with Saying Things Other Candidates Can't," *The Washington Post*, March 9, 2016, https://www.washingtonpost.com/posteverything/wp/2016/03/09/how-donald-trump-gets-away-with-saying-things-other-candidates-cant/?utm_term=.b12706595967.

16   Jonathan Capehart, "Three Ways Donald Trump Has Changed Politics," *The Washington Post*, September 2, 2015, https://www.washingtonpost.com/blogs/post-partisan/wp/2015/09/02/three-ways-donald-trump-has-changed-politics/?utm_term=.26ee3889c531.

17   David Martosko and Nikki Schwab, "'Romney Would Have Dropped to His Knees to Get My Endorsement in 2012': Trump's Amazing 'Sexual' Slur After Former Candidate Brands Him a Conman and a Fraud," *DailyMail.com*, March 3, 2016, http://www.dailymail.co.uk/news/article-3474724/Donald-Trump-phony-fraud-playing-American-public-suckers-Mitt-Romney-throttle-against-GOP-frontrunner-today.html.

18   Gregory Krieg, "Donald Trump Defends the Size of His Penis," *CNN.com*, March 4, 2016, http://www.cnn.com/2016/03/03/politics/donald-trump-small-hands-marco-rubio/.

19   What follows is my deliberately simplified elaboration of Lacan's theories. For more pointed, sophisticated, and scholarly elaborations, see especially Bruce Fink, *A Clinical Introduction to Lacanian Psychoanalysis: Theory and Technique* (Cambridge, MA: Harvard University Press, 1997); and Stephanie Swales, *Perversion: A Lacanian Perspective* (New York: Routledge, 2012).

20   Sabrina Siddiqui, "Donald Trump Pleads Ignorance to Megyn Kelly Over 'Bimbo' Tweets: 'Did I Say That?'" *The Guardian*, May 18, 2016,

https://www.theguardian.com/us-news/2016/may/17/megyn-kelly-trump-interview-bimbo-tweet.

21 Image featured in Liam Stack, "Donald Trump Featured Paula Jones and 2 Other Women Who Accused Bill Clinton of Sexual Assault," *New York Times*, October 9, 2016, https://www.nytimes.com/2016/10/10/us/politics/bill-clinton-accusers.html.

22 Gabriel Sherman, "How Donald Trump Decided to Make Bill Clinton's Accusers a Campaign Issue," *New York Magazine*, October 12, 2016, http://nymag.com/daily/intelligencer/2016/10/how-trump-decided-to-make-clinton-accusers-a-campaign-issue.html.

23 Dan Merica, "Trump Says Both Sides to Blame Amid Charlottesville Backlash," *CNN.com*, August 16, 2017, http://www.cnn.com/2017/08/15/politics/trump-charlottesville-delay/index.html.

24 For an academic explanation of posthumanism, see Joshua Gunn, "Mourning Humanism, or, the Idiom of Haunting," *Quarterly Journal of Speech* 92 (2006): 77–102.

Jennifer R. Mercieca

Afterword: Trump as Anarchist and Sun King

As the essays in this book demonstrate, Donald Trump's 2016 election to the presidency of the United States was a political rupture—it represented a break with traditional presidential campaign rhetoric as well as a break with a traditional presidency. Yet, according to political science "fundamentals" Trump *should* have won the presidency. 2016 was supposed to be a change election because the presidency had been held by the same party for two terms, the economy wasn't so great, and more Americans thought the nation was "on the wrong track" than thought that it was "on the right track."[1] Being a change election, any Republican Party nominee should have defeated any Democratic Party nominee—no matter who the parties nominated. Based upon that analysis Trump's election wasn't disruptive at all, he even underperformed compared to what another Republican nominee might have done. So, why then did Trump's election *seem* so disruptive?

Being a historian of American political rhetoric, I see current politics through the frame of history. We might note at the outset that embedded within Trump's campaign rhetoric is a view of history—his campaign slogan "Make America Great Again" was inherently nostalgic (from the ancient Greek *nostos algia*, meaning "return home"). The most optimistic history of the Trump election would tell the story of how Trump's campaign appealed to those Americans who had a longing for a "return home" to an America from a different time—a time when America was "winning," when "political correctness" did not trump free speech, and a time, perhaps, when things seemed simpler or safer.[2] The less optimistic history of the Trump election would tell the story of how Trump appealed to Americans who held misogynist and racist opinions, of Americans who had a longing for a "return home" to a time in America when it was dominated by white male privilege.

Which of these stories of the Trump rupture will history remember? I suspect that both stories will eventually be told in an attempt to make sense of the Trump election. That Trump's campaign theme was nostalgic is obvious, but what can we say about the implications of its view of history as a political program?

Historian Hayden White gives us a useful way to think about how the embedded views of history in public discourse reveal a political program related to change. He explains that within all historical narratives—including, I believe, the one embedded in Trump's "Make America Great Again" campaign—we find "different conceptions of the desirability of maintaining or changing the social status quo" as well as "different time orientations (an orientation toward past, present, or future as the repository of a paradigm of society's 'ideal' form)." According to White there are four orientations towards the possibility of achieving utopia through political change: anarchist, conservative, radical, and liberal.[3] Very briefly, anarchists "are inclined to idealize a remote past of natural-human innocence from which men have fallen into the corrupt 'social' state in which they currently find themselves"; conservatives "are inclined to imagine historical evolution as a progressive elaboration of the institutional structure that currently prevails, which structure they regard as 'utopia'"; radicals "are inclined to view the utopian condition as imminent, which inspires their concern with the provision of the revolutionary means to bring this utopia to pass now"; and, liberals "project this utopian condition into the remote future, in such a way as to discourage any effort in the present to realize it precipitately, by 'radical' means."[4] Locating utopia in different times and systems leads anarchists and radicals to want to change the current political system, and leads conservatives and liberals to want to maintain it.

According to White's typology Trump's 2016 campaign was anarchy—it longed for a distant past outside of the current system. Trump argued repeatedly that the current American political system had to be destroyed because it had been corrupted by weak and ineffective politicians. He asked Americans to return to a simpler time when the federal government wasn't so big, regulations weren't so tough, and capitalists and capitalism were free. So doing, he promised, would restore American greatness. This represents a startling rupture in American political discourse. Since Franklin Delano Roosevelt's presidency our public discourse has been largely liberal—that is, despite political party, we've seen politicians argue for the stability of the system and incremental changes within the system to bring about their desired programs and policies. For generations, the American economic system and the American political system have been believed to be the best guarantors of freedom, equality, and justice (for most) and so have been unquestioned and unquestionable by mainstream political candidates. Trump questioned the long dominant liberal view of history. Trump's political campaign was illiberal; it was, in fact, anarchic. But, was Trump really an anarchist? If so, what long lost period of American history did Trump idealize and seek to recover?

The news coming out of Trump's March 25, 2016 interview with the *New York Times'* David Sanger and Maggie Haberman was that his foreign policy would be "America first."[5] But, perhaps we ought to have paid a little more attention to one of the questions Haberman posed to Trump on that day.[6] She asked him when he thought that America was greatest? He answered that he thought that America was at its greatest during the Gilded Age at the turn of the twentieth century— before the Progressive Era reforms that would protect the people from the abuse of corrupt corporations and elected officials. Trump, as it turned out, idealized the period in American history right before the liberal view of history took hold among American politicians. Trump didn't say that he was in favor of corruption, of course, he said instead that he admired the Gilded Age because of its unrestrained economic growth — it was a "pretty wild time," Trump thought.[7]

Why the Gilded Age? Trump isn't a fan of restraints, particularly restraints on himself. Trump is a fan of gilding — of adding a thin layer of gold or gold colored stuff to things to make them appear to be more valuable than they are.[8] Gold gilding is the signature design feature of Trump-branded properties and products worldwide.[9] According to Trump's decorator Angelo Donghia, his New York City apartment was designed as a gilded golden tribute to France's Louis XIV — the Sun King who once (perhaps, but maybe not) declared to his Parliament *"l'état, c'est moi"* — I am the state — in defiance of its attempt to restrain him.[10] Trump has lived his life as a Sun King of sorts — he has believed himself to be above the law, never permitting himself to be held accountable for his actions.[11] In fact, Trump takes pride in his Sun King-like ability to decide what is and what is not. "The Golden Rule of Negotiating," Trump once tweeted to his followers, is "he who has the gold makes the rules."[12]

Trump's gilded Sun King *ethos* isn't just for negotiating, politics, or history. It belies his approach to rhetoric as well — instrumental, fake, unaccountable. Trump, believing he has the gold, made his own rules. His presidential campaign used rhetoric strategically — without regard to ethics — to help him to get what he wanted. He used rhetoric to intimidate, to over-whelm, to mock, to threaten, as well as to entertain. Trump weaponized rhetoric to disrupt the liberal consensus, which means that his rhetorical style was anarchic as well.

Of course, during normal presidential campaigns when the liberal view of history prevailed presidential candidates and presidents wanted to win and attempted to use rhetoric to set the nation's agenda, argue for their preferred policies, consti-tute the people, establish the power of the Executive Branch and a whole host of other things, but they didn't use rhetoric with impunity — they weren't anarchists.[13]

Perhaps, Trump's disruptive rhetoric, as Joshua Gunn argued, is truly "perverse" in the sense that it was "a deliberate and knowing deviation from assumed 'norms'." Despite the soundness of political science fundamentals, Trump's election feels so disruptive because he weaponized rhetoric to pervert the liberal norms of American politics and American political discourse. Trump is America's gilded anarchist, Sun King president and, since he believes that whoever has the gold makes the rules, he will be very difficult to control.

Notes

1   Daniel W. Drezner, "Why Political Science is Not an Election Casualty," *The Washington Post*, November 15, 2016, https://www.washington post.com/posteverything/wp/2016/11/15/why-political-science-is-not-an-election-casualty/?utm_term=.1ec3bc4170f6. I'm indebted to my political science colleague Joe Ura for this take on the fundamentals.
2   "nostalgia, n.," *Oxford English Dictionary Online*, June 2017, http://www.oed.com/view/Entry/128472.
3   "utopia, n.," *Oxford English Dictionary Online*, June 2017, http://www.oed.com/view/Entry/220784.
4   White, Hayden V., *Metahistory: The Historical Imagination in Nineteenth-Century Europe* (Baltimore, MD: Johns Hopkins University Press, 1973): 25.
5   David E. Sanger and Maggie Haberman, "In Donald Trump's World-view, America Comes First, and Everybody Else Pays," *New York Times*, March 26, 2016, https://www.nytimes.com/2016/03/27/us/politics/donald-trump-foreign-policy.html?_r=2.
6   Haberman actually asked, "What is the era when you think the United States last had the right balance, either in terms of defense footprint or in terms of trade?" The transcript subheading listed it as a discussion of "When America Was 'Great'": "Transcript: Donald Trump Expounds on His Foreign Policy Views," *New York Times*, March 26, 2016, https://www.nytimes.com/2016/03/27/us/politics/donald-trump-transcript.html.
7   "No if you really look at it, it was the turn of the century, that's when we were a great, when we were really starting to go robust. But if you look back, it really was, there was a period of time when we were developing at the turn of the century which was a pretty wild time for this country and pretty wild in terms of building that machine, that machine was really based on entrepreneurship, etc, etc." "Transcript: Donald Trump Expounds on His Foreign Policy Views."
8   "gilded, adj.," *Oxford English Dictionary Online*, June 2017, http://www.oed.com/view/Entry/78269.

9 Alissa Walker, "An Architectural Tour of Donald Trump's Gaudy Ass
   Skyscrapers," *Gizmodo*, March 03, 2016; Lyndsey Matthews, "A Psychol-
   ogist Reveals What Trump's Fixation with Gold Really Means," *Marie
   Claire*, October 07, 2017, http://www.marieclaire.com/politics/a24996/
   president-trump-gold-obsession-meaning/.

10 Herbert H. Rowen, "'L'Etat C'est a Moi': Louis XIV and the State,"
   French Historical Studies 2.1 (1961): 83–98; Jennifer Fernandez, "Donald
   Trump's 1985 Apartment Looks Exactly How You'd Imagine It," *Architectural Digest*, July 27, 2016, https://www.architecturaldigest.com/
   story/donald-trump-1985-apartment-looks-exactly-how-youd-imagine-
   it; Robert Wellington, "Going for Gold: Trump, Louis XIV and Interior
   Design," *The Conversation*, January 22, 2017, https://theconversation.
   com/going-for-gold-trump-louis-xiv-and-interior-design-71698; Dan
   Evon, "Golden Throne of Lies," *Snopes.com*, August 14, 2016, https://
   www.snopes.com/donald-trumps-golden-toilet/.

11 Or, Trump acts with "impunity" as Davis Houck observes in his
   chapter in this volume, based on Brian Beutler's November 2016 *New
   Republic* article. Brian Beutler, "This Single Concept Explains Trump's
   Many Outrages," *New Republic*, November 23, 2016, https://new
   republic.com/article/138975/single-concept-explains-trumps-many-
   outrages.

12 Donald J. Trump, Twitter post, July 30, 2013, https://twitter.com/real
   donaldtrump/status/362218621428187137.

13 For typical uses of presidential rhetoric see Karlyn Kohrs Campbell and
   Kathleen Hall Jamieson, *Presidents Creating the Presidency: Deeds Done in
   Words* (Chicago, IL: University of Chicago Press, 2008).

Contributors

Dr. Paul J. Achter is associate professor and chair of the rhetoric and communication studies department at the University of Richmond. Dr. Achter studies rhetoric and its connections to television and American political culture, as well as racism, war, and terrorism. He has presented research about Trump and rhetoric and has been cited in articles about Trump's campaign rhetoric in RollCall.com and Politifact. Dr. Achter has published extensively in academic journals and book collections, has won more than half a million dollars in international grants to study television and politics, and has published articles with CNN.com, *The Huffington Post*, and *Salon*.

Dr. Ira Allen is an assistant professor of rhetoric, writing, and digital media studies at Northern Arizona University, where he studies and writes about rhetoric, religion, and politics. He has published multiple scholarly articles, book chapters, and translations, and his book about political rhetoric, freedom, and ethics — *The Ethical Fantasy of Rhetorical Theory* — is forthcoming from the University of Pittsburgh Press. Dr. Allen has a wide international network as a result of collaborations with scholars in Europe and the Middle East.

Dr. Collin Gifford Brooke is an associate professor of rhetoric and writing at Syracuse University. Dr. Brooke is author of the award-winning *Lingua Fracta: Towards a Rhetoric of New Media* (Hampton Press, 2009) and editor of the forthcoming *Rhetoric, Writing, and Circulation* (Utah State University Press, 2018). Dr.

Brooke studies rhetoric and social media, technology, virality, and online networks.

Dr. Joshua Gunn is an associate professor of rhetoric and communication studies at the University of Texas at Austin. Dr. Gunn draws on psychoanalytic theory, especially that of Jacques Lacan, Sigmund Freud, and Julia Kristeva, for a useful vocabulary to make sense of objects and experiences that are (or at least seem) incommunicable. He is the author of over 70 essays and book chapters on rhetoric, media, and cultural studies, as well as *Modern Occult Rhetoric: Mass Media and the Drama of Secrecy in the Twentieth Century* (University of Alabama Press, 2005) and *Speech Craft: Public Speaking in the 21st Century* (Bedford/St. Martin's Press, 2017).

Dr. Davis W. Houck is the Fannie Lou Hamer Endowed Professor of Rhetorical Studies at Florida State University. Dr. Houck is a leading scholar of Presidential and Civil Rights rhetoric and the author/editor of 12 books including the critically acclaimed two-volume compilation of Civil Rights documents, *Rhetoric, Religion, and the Civil Rights Movement, 1954–1965* (Baylor University Press, 2006, 2014), *The Speeches of Fannie Lou Hamer: To Tell It Like It Is* (University Press of Mississippi, 2011), and *Emmett Till and the Mississippi Press* (University Press of Mississippi, 2008). He has also worked on several documentary film projects, including TVOne's series, *Murder in Black and White* (2008), and *Fannie Lou Hamer's America* (in production). Dr. Houck was recently profiled on NPR, NPR affiliates, and elsewhere for his efforts to establish the Emmett Till Research Archive at Florida State University in 2016.

Dr. Jennifer R. Mercieca is an associate professor of rhetoric at Texas A&M University. She studies American political discourse, especially as it relates to citizenship, democracy, and the presidency, and she is the Director of the Aggie Agora, which is a non-profit, non-partisan critical thinking and citizen engagement program in the College of Liberal Arts at Texas A&M. Dr. Mercieca has published two books about political rhetoric, *Founding Fictions* (University of Alabama Press, 2010) and *The Rhetoric of Heroic Expectations: Establishing the Obama Presidency* (Texas A&M University Press, 2014), and she is working on a new book about Donald Trump's political rhetoric and demagoguery. Her articles about Trump and the 2016 election have been published in *USA Today*, *The Huffington Post*, *Politico*, *The Conversation*, and other major media outlets and have been viewed more than 250,000 times. She has also been interviewed about Trump's rhetoric by the *BBC World News*, *The New York Times*, *Le Monde*, *Slate*, and other media outlets, and she was featured on NPR's 2016 Inauguration episode of "All Things Considered."

Dr. Patricia Roberts-Miller is a professor of rhetoric at the University of Texas at Austin and has published four books about rhetoric, political theory, and public policy, including *Voices in the Wilderness: Public Discourse and the Paradox of Puritan Rhetoric* (University Alabama Press, 1999), *Deliberate Conflict: Argument, Political Theory, and Composition Classes* (Southern Illinois University Press, 2007), and *Fanatical Schemes: Proslavery Rhetoric and the Tragedy of Consensus* (University Alabama Press, 2010). She is an internationally recognized expert on rhetoric, hate speech, and authoritarianism, and recently published a trade book about demagoguery, *Demagoguery and Democracy* (The Experiment, 2017).

Dr. Ryan Skinnell is an assistant professor of rhetoric and writing at San José State University. He is the author of *Conceding Composition: A Crooked History of Composition's Institutional Fortunes* (Utah State University Press, 2016), along with numerous journal articles and book chapters. He is the review editor for *Present Tense: A Journal for Rhetoric in Society* and has co-edited three books: *What We Wish We'd Known: Negotiating Graduate School* (Fountainhead Press, 2015), *Bureaucracy: A Love Story* (Aquiline Books, 2018), and *Reinventing (with) Theory in Rhetoric & Writing Studies* (under review). Dr. Skinnell has written about Donald Trump's rhetoric for *Washington Monthly* and the *University Press of Colorado Blog*.

Dr. Michael J. Steudeman is assistant professor of rhetoric at Penn State University. His scholarship examines the rhetoric of public education as a response to social problems in the United States. He also studies the history of American public address, particularly how presidential candidates present their identities in the midst of presidential campaigns. His work has been published in academic journals including *Rhetoric & Public Affairs*, *Communication Quarterly*, and *The Quarterly Journal of Speech*.

Dr. Jennifer Wingard is an associate professor of rhetoric, composition, and pedagogy at the University of Houston. She studies rhetoric, citizenship, and neoliberal economics and is the author of *Branded Bodies, Rhetoric, and the Neoliberal Nation-State* (Lexington Books, 2013). She has been interviewed as an expert on Trump's rhetoric for stories published in *USA Today*, *The Washington Post*, *ProPublica*, *Pacific Standard*, and other outlets, and she published "What Trump's Rhetoric Says About His Leadership" on *Fortune.com* immediately after the election.

Dr. Anna M. Young is an associate professor and chair of communication and theater at Pacific Lutheran University. Dr. Young studies rhetorical style, expertise, and public relations. She is the author of *Prophets, Gurus, and Pundits: Rhetorical Styles and Public Engagement* (Southern Illinois University Press, 2014) and editor of *Teacher, Scholar, Mother: Re-Envisioning Motherhood in the Academy* (Lexington Books, 2015).

Acknowledgments

Academics are writers by trade. We are trained to write as part of our careers, and many of us find considerable satisfaction in the task. But as every writer knows, even when you have a lot of practice writing and are eager to undertake a particular writing challenge, it can still be tough sledding when you have to produce a different kind of writing for new audiences than you're used to. Doing it successfully requires a lot of goodwill, support, and feedback from other people.

In the case of a book like this one — in which we are trying to translate our disciplinary expertise into language that non-experts can reasonably understand — that goodwill, support, and feedback often comes from people who are not pre-disposed to understanding what academics traditionally write. In other words, a lot of people who didn't have to did a lot of work to help us out. Such was the case with this book, and it was no small effort on their parts to make enough sense of what we wrote in order to offer improvements. The people who provided the support and feedback deserve all the more credit for their goodwill and contributions. As a result, there is a laundry list of people who deserve mention for making this book possible — and more importantly, readable.

I join this book's contributors in thanking the following people, who read proposals, introductions, and chapters — sometimes more than once — and offered crucial feedback with grace and discernment: Andrea Alden, Xochilt Almendarez, Aidan Boatman, Cameron Brown, Barry Brummett, Raymond Caballero, Anthony Diaz, Cristyn Elder, Melissa Finefrock, Jennifer Forester, Kaitlin Graves, Michael Gray, Rod Hart,

Johanna Hartelius, Michael Helfield, Daniel Hendel De La O, Mary Hull Caballero, Jeffrey Isaac, Rachel Elizabeth Khoriander, Bonnie Lenore Kyburz, Barbara L'Eplattenier, Emily Lanigan, Tye Lewin, Degan Loren, Jake Meth, Thomas Moriarty, Laura Noll, Anne Skinnell, Charie Skinnell, Robert Skinnell, Damariyé Smith, Jonathan Smith, Nick Taylor, and Tim Weyel.

Additionally, I'd like to thank some other generous people who made this book possible. Collin Gifford Brooke organized the conference panel in 2017 that was the impetus for this book, and he didn't cry foul when I asked to pick up and extend what began as his idea. At various points, Ira Allen, Joshua Gunn, Angela Haas, Jennifer Mercieca, Alex Parrish, Rachel Schmidt-Rocha, Nick Taylor, and Jennifer Wingard answered my flustered calls for help and put me in touch with helpful people — editors, agents, contributors — who made the materials better and made the book possible. Charie Skinnell vetted the book's title (or more importantly, weeded out a bunch of previous — not so good — titles). Eric Detweiler designed the book cover, apparently without really even realizing how good it was, and offered it freely. Geoffrey Clegg and Rachel Elizabeth Khoriander provided Latin translation advice. Eli Current provided crucial editing assistance. Andrea Alden, Megan Alfaro, Ariel Andrew, Cynthia Baer, Don Bialostosky, Forrest Cook, Danielle Deveau, Stephen Domingo, Christopher Forkin, Irma Garcia, Kendall Gerdes, Eli Hansen, Matthew Heard, Jason Helms, Judy Holiday, Linda Hull, Robert James, Jennifer Johnson, Matthew Keast, Jeff Klausman, Kelan Koning, Bonnie Lenore Kyburz, Jonathan Lovell, Heather Luther, Katie May, Richard McNabb, Jennifer Mercieca, Helen Meservey, Cathleen Miller, Linda Mitchell, Tommy Mouton, Jillian Murphy, Amber Norwood, Katherine O'Meara, Dawn Opel, Lisa Parham, Jada Patchigondla, Donnie Johnson Sackey, Sweeney Schragg, Namita Singhal, Boris Slager, Josh Speers, Mark A. Thompson, and Kelly Wisecup provided invaluable support, feedback, and encouragement at all the right times. There are surely more people who deserve gratitude, and to anyone I may have missed, I offer my sincerest thanks.

Finally, thanks to the good people at Imprint Academic, especially editor Graham Horswell, for their professionalism, generosity, and patience.

Index

CPSIA information can be obtained
at www.ICGtesting.com
Printed in the USA
BVOW08s1636180418
513742BV00001B/66/P